ANNUITY
PRINCIPLES AND PRODUCTS

LOMA (Life Office Management Association, Inc.) is an international association founded in 1924. LOMA is committed to a business partnership with its worldwide members in the insurance and financial services industry to improve their management and operations through quality employee development, research, information sharing, and related products and services. Among LOMA's activities is the sponsorship of the FLMI Insurance Education Program—an educational program intended primarily for home office and branch office employees.

The ***Associate, Annuity Products and Administration (AAPA) Program*** is designed for people who work with all areas of annuities—including product development, marketing/sales, administration, customer service, systems, investments, accounting, and legal/compliance—as well as regulators. To earn the AAPA designation, a student must complete all required courses as outlined in LOMA's most current *Insurance Education Catalog*. Upon successful completion of all required courses, the student receives a diploma awarded by LOMA and is entitled to use the letters *AAPA* after his/her name.

ANNUITY

PRINCIPLES and PRODUCTS

John P. Burger, FLMI, ACS

Kristen L. Falk, FLMI, ACS, AIAA

AAPA

LOMA's Associate Annuity Products and Administration Program
Atlanta, Georgia

LOMA
Information that Works

PROJECT TEAM:

Authors:	John P. Burger, FLMI, ACS Kristen L. Falk, FLMI, ACS, AIAA
Project Managers:	Joyce Abrams Fleming, J.D., FLMI, ACS, AIAA, ALHC, HIA, MHP Dean Polk, FLMI, ALHC, ACS
Production/Editorial Manager:	Stephanie Philippo
Exams Editor:	Martha Parker, FLMI, ACS, AIAA, ALHC
Manuscript Editor:	Susan Smith Jones, J.D.
Copyeditor:	Robert D. Land, FLMI, ACS
Permissions Editor:	Michon Wise
Production/Print Coordinator:	Cara Taylor Gaskins
Cover Art and Design:	Score promotion+design The Project Center
Administrative Support:	Aurelia Kennedy-Hemphill
Typography:	DTP Solutions

ISBN 1-57974-073-1

Library of Congress Catalog Card Number: 99-73130

Printed in the United States of America

CONTENTS

Preface ix

Chapter 1: Annuities Defined 2

The Current Environment 3
    The Social Security System 3
    Aging Population 4
    The Stock Market 4
Annuities as Retirement Funding Products 4
The Annuity Contract 5
    Parties to an Annuity Contract 5
Types of Annuities 7
    Immediate and Deferred Annuities 7
    Single-Premium and Flexible-Premium Annuities 8
    Group and Individual Annuities 10
    Qualified and Nonqualified Annuities 10
    Fixed and Variable Annuities 10
    Payout Period Options 11

Chapter 2: The Annuity Contract 14

The Process of Applying for an Annuity Contract 15
    Applicant Information 16
    Contract Ownership 16
    General Provisions of the Contract 17
    Purchase Payments 18
    Free Look Provision 19
The Accumulation Period 19
    Premium Payments 19
    Insurance Company Fees/Charges 21
    Withdrawals 23
    Death Benefit Provisions 25
The Payout Period 25
    Lump Sum Distribution 26
    Fixed Period or Fixed Amount 26
    Annuitization 26
    Fixed and Variable Payout Options 28
    Calculating the Annuity Payment 28

Chapter 3: Fixed and Equity-Indexed Annuities 32

Fixed Annuities 33
   The General Account 33
   Interest Rate Guarantees 33
   Payout Guarantees 34
   Inflation Erosion 35
Equity-Indexed Annuities 35
   The Index 35
   Interest Rate Guarantees 36
   Calculating Excess Interest 36
   Crediting Excess Interest 37
   Other Contract Provisions 38
   Pricing Equity-Indexed Annuities 38
   The Growth of the Equity-Indexed Annuity Market 38

Chapter 4: Variable and Market Value Adjusted Annuities 40

Variable Annuities 41
   Investment Risk and Return 41
   The Separate Account 42
   Subaccounts 43
   Asset Allocation 48
   Special Services 49
   Death Benefit 52
   Payout Period 52
Market Value Adjusted Annuities 55

Chapter 5: Annuities and Investments 58

Dealing with Risk 59
   Investing and Risk Tolerance 60
   Risks Associated with Fixed and
      Equity-Indexed Annuities 62
   Risks Associated with Variable Annuities 63
Investment Principles 64
   The Time Value of Money 64
   Dollar Cost Averaging 64
   Diversification and Asset Allocation 65
Annuities Compared to Other Financial Products 66
   Annuities Compared to Savings Accounts and
      Certificates of Deposit 66
   Annuities Compared to Mutual Funds 67
   Annuities Compared to Stocks and Bonds 69

Chapter 6: Individual and Group Annuities 70

Individual Nonqualified Annuities 71
    Retirement Savings 71
    Lump Sum Distributions 73
    Education Funding 74
Group Retirement Plans and Annuities 75
    Qualified Retirement Plans 76
    Keogh Plans 79
    Simplified Employee Pension Plans 80
    Savings Incentive Match Plan for Employees 80
    Nonqualified Retirement Plans 81

Chapter 7: Taxation of Annuities 84

Income Taxes 85
    Tax Deferral on Investment Income 85
    Deductibility of Premium Payments for the
       Plan Participant 86
    Deductibility of Premium Payments for Owners of IRAs
       and Nonqualified Annuities 87
    Deductibility of Premium Payments for Sponsors of
       Qualified Retirement Plans 88
    Taxation of Annuity Income 89
Estate Taxes 93
Section 1035 Exchanges 94
Rollovers 94
Canadian Taxation of Annuities 95
    Individual Annuities 95
    Retirement Plans 95

Chapter 8: Regulation of the Annuity Industry 98

State Regulation 99
    Solvency Regulation 100
    Market Conduct Regulation 102
Federal Regulation 105
    National Association of Securities Dealers 106
    Suitability 107
    Disclosure 108
    Advertising 109
Equity-Indexed Annuities and Market Value Adjusted
    Annuities 109
Canadian Regulation 110
    Provincial Legislation 110
    Federal Regulation in Canada 111

Chapter 9: Marketing and Distributing Annuities ... 114

Marketing Basics 115
Product Development 116
    Product Planning 117
    Comprehensive Business Analysis 118
    Product Technical Design 119
    Product Implementation 119
    Sales Monitoring and Product Review 120
Product Promotion 120
    Personal Selling 120
    Advertising 121
    Sales Promotion 121
    Publicity 121
Distribution Systems 122
    Personal Selling Distribution Systems 123
    Direct Response Distribution Systems 126
Choosing a Distribution System 127

Chapter 10: The Future of Annuities 130

Societal Developments 131
    Growing Number of Retirees 131
    Lengthening of Retirement 133
Social Security 134
    Modifying Social Security 134
    Establishing Individual Savings or Personal
      Retirement Accounts 134
    Phasing Out Social Security 135
Employer-Sponsored Pension Plans 135
    Encouraging 401(k) Participation 135
    Small Businesses 135
Tax Reform and the Regulation of Annuities 136
    Proposals to Tax 1035 Exchanges 137
    Changes in the Capital Gains Tax 137
    Regulation of Annuities 137
Potential Effects of Change on Annuities 138
    Social Security and Annuities 138
    Employer-Sponsored Retirement Plans and Annuities 138
    How Insurers Respond to Change Through Product
      Design and Marketing 139

Appendix: Sample Annuity Contract 142
Glossary 155
Index 177

PREFACE

The purpose of *Annuity Principles and Products* is to provide an overview of the annuities industry, with a special emphasis on basic concepts and annuity products. This book has been designed for students who are preparing for LOMA's AAPA 273 examination.

Several features have been included in each chapter to help you organize your studies, reinforce your understanding of the materials, and prepare for the examination. As we describe each of these features, we offer suggestions for studying the material.

Learning Objectives. The first page of each chapter contains a list of learning objectives to help you focus your studies. Before reading each chapter, review these learning objectives. Then, as you read the chapter, look for material that will help you meet the learning objectives.

Key Terms and Concepts. The text assumes that you have no previous experience with annuities, so basic terms and concepts are defined and explained. All terminology introduced in this text is defined or explained when it is first used. Important terminology is highlighted in italic, boldface type when the term is first used or defined and is included in a list of key terms and concepts at the end of each chapter. All key terms are also included in a comprehensive glossary at the end of the book; each glossary entry identifies in brackets the number of the chapter in which the term is defined. As you read each chapter pay special attention to the key terms.

Insights. Insights appear throughout the text and are designed to amplify the text's descriptions of certain topics. These Insights should help you get a better feel for how annuities operate and their importance in the context of the insurance and financial services industry.

Test Preparation Guide. Besides this book, LOMA's *Test Preparation Guide for AAPA 273* (Melanie R. Green and Martha Parker, FLMI, ACS, AIAA, ALHC) is assigned reading for students preparing to take the AAPA 273 examination. Used along with this textbook, the Test Preparation Guide will help you master the course material. Included in the Guide are practice exam questions and a full-scale sample examination, along with answers to all the questions.

LOMA recommends that you use the Test Preparation Guide for this course. **Studies indicate that students who use LOMA study aids consistently perform significantly better on LOMA examinations than other students.**

ACKNOWLEDGMENTS

Annuity Principles and Products is the result of the joint efforts of professionals from insurance and financial services industry companies and

LOMA staff. Members of LOMA's Equity Products and Annuity Committee (EPAC) were involved with the project from its inception. They helped to shape the AAPA program, commented on the initial outline for this text, and provided the authors with valuable material and industry perspectives. We appreciate the assistance provided by Michael Jensen, Associate, Operations Management, LOMA, who facilitated our communication with the committee. On behalf of LOMA and its membership, the authors would like to thank the committee for its generous support and encouragement. Many of the members of the committee also graciously volunteered considerable amounts of their time to review the textbook chapters.

Textbook Review Panel

The authors are deeply indebted to the members of the textbook review panel. The source materials, invaluable suggestions and critical evaluations supplied by the reviewers were essential to the book's accuracy and completeness.

Paula Boswell Beier, FLMI, ACS
Account Executive, Relationship Management
Outsourcing Solutions Division of NaviSys

Paige C. Clark
Director, Annuity Operations
Horace Mann Life Insurance Company

Constance A. Doern, FLMI
Vice President—Policy Services
Cova Life Administration Services Company

Carol Ann Detlef, CLU, FLMI
Director—Annuity Administration
Northwestern Mutual Life

Sandra Fox, Vice President
Annuity Product Development
Prudential Investments

Elizabeth Gottfried, FLMI, ACS
Product and Compliance Consultant
Outsourcing Solutions Division of NaviSys

Michael R. Hood
Financial Services Associate
American General Financial Group

Barbara A. O'Rourke, ACS
Variable Products Manager
CUNA Mutual Life Insurance Company

Audrey Paulsen
Variable Products Specialist
Allianz Life Insurance Company of North America

Diana Scheel, FLMI, ACS, CLU, ChFC
Executive Director, Life/Annuity Claims, Benefits & Analysis
USAA Life Company

Teresa Shumila, FLMI, ACS
Assistant Vice President, Distribution and Client Services
Keyport Life Insurance Company

David J. Tobin, CPA, FLMI
Senior Vice President and COO
Templeton Funds Annuity Company

Linda T. Weinstein, FLMI, ACS, CEBS
Senior Business Strategist
Lincoln National Life Insurance Company

Dan Werner, FLMI, CLU, ChFC
Assistant Director, Individual Compliance
The Principal

Besides the members of the textbook review panel, other insurance and financial services professionals provided feedback on the program, course outline, or individual chapters. We would like to thank the following companies and individuals:

◆ ARM Financial Group (William H. Guth, CLU, ChFC, Vice President, Product Development)
◆ CUNA Mutual Life Insurance Company (Kathy Koppedryer, FLMI, ACS, Benefit Specialist)
◆ Fidelity Investments Life Insurance Company (Lisa Glass, Trainer)
◆ The Hartford (Patricia Kurlansky, AVP, Individual Annuity Department; Rosalie Christensen, Sr. Education Specialist; Sonja Fuller, Education Specialist; Sue Hilborn, Education Specialist)
◆ Horace Mann Life Insurance Company (Bill Kelly, Vice President-Annuity Administration and Compliance)
◆ Massachusetts Mutual Life Insurance Company (Michael P. Drees, FLMI, Second Vice President)
◆ Met Life (Betsy Davis, Vice President, Client Administration)
◆ The MONY Group (Terry Hoffman-DeWitt, ACS, Assistant Vice President, Policyholder Services-Variable Products)
◆ NaviSys (Pat Ellis, Vice President, Life and Annuity Services, Outsourcing Solutions Division and Bruce Shoults, Director, Individual Annuities and Telecommunications, Outsourcing Solutions Division)
◆ Northwestern Mutual Life (Herbert J. Kretzer, Senior Marketing Specialist, and John Wozniak, CPA, FLMI, Tax Reporting Coordinator)
◆ Prudential Investments (Keith Hylind, CLU, Director, Annuity Services)

LOMA Staff/Consultants

As is the case with all textbooks developed by LOMA, *Annuity Principles and Products* required the dedicated teamwork of a number of LOMA staff members and consultants. LOMA texts, including *Intro to Annuities*, *Life and Health Insurance Marketing*, and *Regulatory Compliance: Insurance and Annuity Products*, proved to be valuable background materials for the authors. Aurelia K. Hemphill, Administrative Assistant, Insurance & Financial Services Programs (IFSP), provided administrative support for the project. Cara Taylor Gaskins, Production Coordinator, coordinated the layout of the text and made all printing arrangements. Michon Wise, Editorial/Permissions Coordinator copyedited portions of the text and obtained the permissions for use of copyrighted material. Robert D. Land, FLMI, ACS, copyedited the text. Stephanie Philippo, Director, Editorial/ Production/Intellectual Property Management, managed the editing, typesetting, and design of the book. Tom Lundin, FLMI, ACS, AIAA, PAHM, Associate, IFSP, reviewed portions of the manuscript. Susan Smith Jones, J.D., served as manuscript editor for the project. Martha Parker, FLMI, ACS, AIAA, ALHC, Senior Associate, Examinations, reviewed the manuscript and made many valuable suggestions. Jena L. Kennedy, FLMI, ACS, ALHC, CLU, PAHM, Director, Managed Healthcare Programs championed the program and the text during the planning stages.

Special thanks go to Joyce Abrams Fleming, J.D., FLMI, ACS, AIAA, ALHC, HIA, MHP, Director, IFSP, who edited all chapters and supervised the project, making many improvements to the text in the process. The support of Dennis W. Goodwin, FLMI, ACS, HIA, Assistant Vice President, IFSP, and William H. Rabel, Ph.D., FLMI, CLU, Senior Vice President, Education Division, was instrumental to the success of the project.

John P. Burger, FLMI, ACS
Kristen L. Falk, FLMI, ACS, AIAA
Atlanta, Georgia
1999

CHAPTER 1

Annuities Defined

After studying this chapter, you should be able to

◆ Describe the purpose of an annuity

◆ Define the key terms *insurer, contract owner, non-natural owner, annuitant, joint annuitant, beneficiary,* and *accumulation period*

◆ Identify and discuss the common types of annuities

During the past decade, personal financial planning, retirement planning, and the related financial products that are available have become increasingly important to the U.S. population. One financial product for funding retirement that has enjoyed considerable popularity in recent years is the annuity. In the financial services industry, an *annuity* is a contract under which an insurance company promises to make a series of periodic payments to a named person in exchange for a premium or a series of premiums.

Historically, only insurance companies were allowed to issue and sell annuities, because issuing annuities requires specialized expertise and involves considerable financial risk, which is the hallmark of insurance. Today, however, banks, stockbrokers, savings and loan institutions, and other financial services providers can *sell* annuity products, but only insurance companies can *issue* annuities. And so, throughout this text, we will refer to companies that sell and issue annuities—and distribute annuity payments—as insurers.

In this chapter, we provide (1) a general overview of annuities in the context of the current financial services environment and (2) some basic terminology essential for understanding the discussions of annuities in the rest of the text. We will introduce three factors that have contributed to increased interest in planning for retirement and retirement funding products. Then we discuss annuities as retirement funding vehicles.

THE CURRENT ENVIRONMENT

As we mentioned earlier, financial and retirement planning and annuity products have become increasingly popular in the United States. At least three factors in the broad financial services environment have contributed to this increased interest: concerns about the future of the Social Security system, the aging of the U.S. population, and the performance of the U.S. stock market. In this section, we will briefly discuss each of these factors as they relate to increased interest in annuities.

The Social Security System

Retirement planning experts and consumers alike are concerned that the Social Security system may be unable to provide its present level of benefits to future retirees as the percentage of the population receiving benefits increases.

In fact, an ongoing debate in the U.S. Congress during the last few years has involved overhauling or "saving" Social Security. Whatever the outcome of this debate, experts agree that most people who hope to live comfortably in retirement will not be able to do so if they depend solely on Social Security benefits and payments from an employer-sponsored pension plan.

Aging Population

Another important factor that has contributed to an increasing interest in retirement planning is the aging of the U.S. population. Baby boomers are turning 50, an age when many people become much more serious about planning for retirement, an event that no longer seems as remote to them as it once may have. In addition, baby boomers will live longer than previous generations and will need additional financial resources to provide a high quality of life.

The Stock Market

A third factor that has increased interest in personal financial planning, in addition to retirement planning, has been the extraordinarily positive performance of the U.S. stock market over the last decade. Despite the dramatic increase in the number of people investing in the stock market, this may not be the best choice for many people who wish to invest money intended for their retirement. For those people, variable annuities—which we will discuss in Chapter 4—may provide both the opportunity to invest in the stock market and to defer paying taxes on investment earnings.

ANNUITIES AS RETIREMENT FUNDING PRODUCTS

Later in the text, we will discuss a number of different uses for annuities. However, the traditional and intended function of an annuity is to accumulate funds for retirement. Although numerous factors are responsible for the suitability of annuities for this purpose, two major reasons stand out.

Annuities are sometimes described as the opposite of life insurance because annuities protect against the financial consequences of outliving one's resources, while life insurance protects against the financial problems often associated with premature death. In other words, an annuity provides protection against the possibility that a person will live so long that he will deplete the entire amount of money that he has saved to meet financial obligations in his old age. With an annuity, the financial risk of "living too long" is transferred to an insurance company. Because annuity products possess this unique feature, they have traditionally been sold to provide a continuous stream of retirement income.

Annuities also possess other features—beyond that of simply providing retirement income—that broaden their appeal to consumers. Annuities also provide a means for people to accumulate income on a tax-deferred basis. We will discuss this and many other features of annuities in detail later in the text.

THE ANNUITY CONTRACT

An *annuity contract* is a legally enforceable written agreement under which an insurer promises to make a series of periodic payments to a named person, starting on a specified date, in exchange for a premium or series of premiums paid to the insurer. The terms of the annuity contract govern the rights and duties of the contracting parties.

Parties to an Annuity Contract

The parties to the annuity contract are the insurer that issues the contract and the *contract owner* who applies for and purchases the contract. The annuity contract also specifies the *annuitant* whose lifetime is used to measure the length of time annuity payments are payable under the annuity contract. The *payee* is the person who receives the annuity payments. In most cases, the contract owner, the annuitant, and the payee are all the same person. The *beneficiary* is the person or legal entity that receives the annuity death benefit, if applicable. We'll explain more about annuity death benefits in Chapter 2. Figure 1-1 contains a very general description of an annuity purchase. We will use this figure to illustrate the basic operation of an annuity contract as we continue our discussion of annuities.

FIGURE 1.1

An Annuity Purchase.

Rhonda Jackson, age 50, pays $50,000 to Long Life Insurance Company for the purchase of an annuity. Long Life promises to pay Ms. Jackson a specified dollar amount per month beginning on her 65th birthday, about 15 years from the date of purchase, and continuing for the rest of her life. If Ms. Jackson should die before her 65th birthday—when the annuity payments are scheduled to begin—Long Life will pay a specified death benefit to Ms. Jackson's sister, Linda.

Insurer

As we stated before, although many types of institutions sell or distribute annuities, only insurance companies can issue annuity contracts. Therefore, even if a person buys an annuity through a bank or a stockbroker, an insurer will eventually receive the premium and an insurer will be responsible for making the annuity payments or paying the death benefits when they come due.

When an insurer issues an annuity contract, it accepts either a single premium or a series of premiums from the contract owner. Under the annuity contract, the insurer has the duty to make annuity payments according to the terms of the contract. It also promises to pay the beneficiary any death benefit, if applicable. In our example in Figure 1-1, Long Life accepted a single premium of $50,000 from Ms. Jackson. Long Life's duty, then, is to make the annuity payments to Ms. Jackson beginning on her 65th birthday, as the annuity contract specifies. It also promises to pay a death benefit to Ms. Jackson's sister, if Ms. Jackson dies before she reaches age 65. We will discuss annuity contracts and the provisions that they contain further in the next chapter.

Contract Owner

As defined earlier, the annuity contract owner is the person or entity that applies for and purchases the annuity. In our illustration, Rhonda Jackson is the contract owner. The contract owner can be a real person or may be an entity such as a trust, a partnership, or a corporation. A contract owner who is not a person is often called a **non-natural owner**. If the contract owner pays the annuity premiums to the insurer according to the provisions of the contract, then the insurer is obligated to make the annuity payments.

The contract owner has a number of rights under the annuity contract. The contract owner selects the annuitant and designates the beneficiary. The contract owner is also entitled to determine at what point the annuity payments will begin. In our example, Ms. Jackson designated her sister as beneficiary. Ms. Jackson also chose to have the annuity payments begin on her 65th birthday. Some other rights of the contract owner may include the right to cancel the contract and receive a refund (minus any applicable charges) before payments begin, the right to add or withdraw money from the annuity, the right to change the beneficiary, the right to change the ownership of the contract, and, in some instances, the right to assign the annuity contract to another person or entity.

Annuitant

In many cases, the length of time that annuity payments are made is determined by how long the annuitant lives; generally, as long as the annuitant is still alive, the annuity payments continue. Under some payment options, when that person dies, the payments end. In most cases, and in the example of Ms. Jackson, the contract owner and the annuitant are the same person. If the annuitant is someone other than the contract owner, then generally that annuitant has no rights under the annuity contract. Because the annuitant's life expectancy is used as the measure of the annuity, the annuitant must be a natural person—not a legal entity such as a trust or partnership.

At the time an annuity contract is issued, the annuitant generally must not be older than a specific maximum age—typically between 70 and 85—set by the insurer. Some insurers require an annuitant to be under the age of 75 when the annuity contract is formed, while others allow annuitants to be up to 85 years old. In some states, the maximum age limit is specified in state regulations.

Joint Annuitant

The contract owner can also purchase an annuity that names more than one annuitant. That second person is known as a **joint annuitant**. Both the annuitant's and the joint annuitant's ages and life expectancies are used in the calculations to determine what the annuity payments will be.

Beneficiary

When the contract owner dies before annuity payments begin, the insurer is obligated by the terms of most annuity contracts to pay death benefits to a named annuity *beneficiary*. The contract owner can name any natural person or legal entity as beneficiary of the death benefit. In Figure 1-1, Ms. Jackson named her sister as her beneficiary but she could have named any person or entity she desired, including a trust, or even her estate. The annuity beneficiary has no rights under the annuity contract except to receive the death benefit, and, in most cases, the contract owner may change the beneficiary designation on the annuity contract at any time. We will learn more about the beneficiary's right to receive death benefits in Chapter 2.

TYPES OF ANNUITIES

Any particular annuity product can be classified in several different ways, depending on when payments are to begin, how premiums are paid, how premiums are taxed, how contributions are invested, and the type of payout option chosen. The next section provides an overview of the major annuity classifications. Some of the classifications introduced in the next section will be discussed in much greater detail later in the text.

Immediate and Deferred Annuities

One way of differentiating among annuities is by looking at when payments begin. An annuity can be classified as either an immediate annuity or a deferred annuity, depending on when the insurer begins making periodic annuity payments.

In an **immediate annuity**, payments generally are scheduled to begin one annuity period after the date on which the annuity was issued. An **annuity period** is the time span between each of the payments in the series of periodic annuity payments. The annuity period is typically either one month or one year, but other payment options, such as quarterly or semi-annually, are also available. For example, an annuity that provides for a series of annual payments has an annuity period of one year and is referred to as an *annual annuity*. If Dawn Carter purchases an immediate annuity with an annual annuity period in October of 1999, then the insurer will begin making annuity payments in October of 2000. An annuity that provides for an annuity period of one month is referred to as a *monthly annuity*; a monthly immediate annuity will generate its first payment one month after a single premium is paid.

A *deferred annuity* is one under which periodic payments generally are scheduled to begin more than one annuity period after the date on which the annuity was purchased. In the example of the annuity purchase described in Figure 1-1, Rhonda Jackson had purchased a deferred annuity. People often purchase deferred annuities during their working years in anticipation of the need for retirement income later in their lives. Although a deferred annuity typically specifies the date on which payments are scheduled to begin, depending upon state requirements, the contract owner usually can change this date at any time before the first payment is made.

The time period between the date that the contract owner purchases the annuity and the date that payments begin is known as the *accumulation period*. Once payments begin, the annuity is said to be in the *payout period*. Immediate annuities have no accumulation period, because annuity payments begin within one annuity period. Figure 1-2 shows the accumulation period and payout period for a deferred annuity.

FIGURE 1.2

Accumulation Period of a Deferred Annuity.

Contract owner pays 10 annual premiums for an annuity

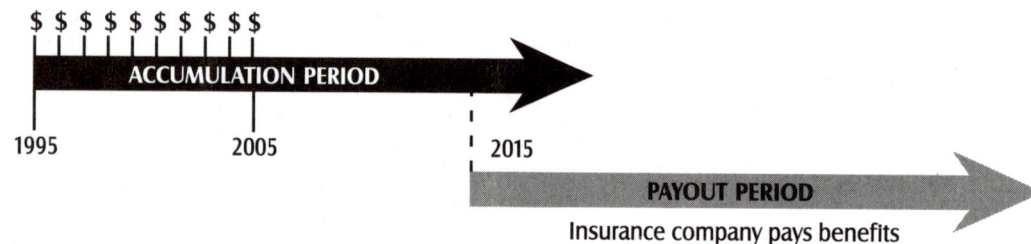

$ $ $ $ $ $ $ $ $

ACCUMULATION PERIOD

1995   2005   2015

PAYOUT PERIOD
Insurance company pays benefits

Single-Premium and Flexible-Premium Annuities

When a contract owner purchases an annuity, she may choose to pay the premium in one lump sum or a series of premium payments. The function of an annuity is basically the same regardless of whether the premium is paid in one sum or in a series of payments. The premium payment method, however, affects the length of time that the insurer holds the premium payments. Under most circumstances, the longer the insurer holds a given premium, the larger will be the earnings generated by that premium.

Single-Premium Annuities

As the name suggests, a *single-premium annuity* is an annuity that is purchased by the payment of one lump sum premium. Because payments begin soon after an immediate annuity is purchased, an immediate annuity is purchased with a single premium; such an annuity is known as a *single-premium immediate annuity (SPIA)*. The purpose of an SPIA is to convert a lump sum payment into an income stream, making it an attractive vehicle for providing retirement income. SPIAs also can be used to fund life insurance or long-term care insurance premiums, to spread out lottery payments and personal injury settlement payments, and to achieve a variety of estate planning strategies.

Deferred annuities can also be purchased with single premiums. These annuities are called **single-premium deferred annuities (SPDAs)**. The lump sum that is used to purchase the annuity is held by the insurer until such time as the contract owner decides to begin receiving payments. Most insurers will accept additional premiums known as **window premiums** for SPDAs during the first contract year. The distinction between an SPIA and an SPDA is that the payments for the SPDA usually would not begin within the annuity period, for example within the next year.

Flexible-Premium Annuities

In some cases, a person who wants to purchase an annuity might not have a large lump sum of cash with which to purchase the annuity. So, this person would make premium payments over a period of months or years. Under a **flexible-premium annuity**, the contract owner pays premiums on a periodic basis over a stated period of time; the amount of each premium payment, however, can vary between a set minimum amount and a set maximum amount. For example, the contract might allow the contract owner to pay any premium amount between $250 and $10,000 each year. The contract owner can also choose not to pay any premium in a given year; the only requirement is that any premium amount paid each year must fall within the stated minimum and maximum. Note that every annuity purchased with the payment of periodic premiums is by definition a deferred annuity. Figure 1-3 provides a summary of the characteristics of immediate and deferred annuities.

FIGURE 1.3

A Comparison of Immediate and Deferred Annuities.

Immediate Annuity

- Purchased with a single premium.
- No accumulation period. The annuity payments usually begin no later than one year after the annuity is purchased.
- Purpose: To convert a lump sum into an income stream for the contract owner.

Deferred Annuity

- Can be purchased with a single premium or a series of premiums.
- Accumulation period usually lasts for years but is generally at least more than one annuity period after the annuity is purchased.
- Purpose: To provide a means for the contract owner to accumulate funds until a future point in time.

Group and Individual Annuities

Insurers sell annuities on both an individual and a group basis. If a person purchases an individual annuity contract, that person is the owner of that contract. Under a group annuity contract, each person in the specified group receives a certificate indicating that he is participating under the group annuity contract—a separate contract is not issued to each person. In Chapter 6 of this text, we will discuss both group and individual annuities in greater detail.

Qualified and Nonqualified Annuities

You may have read about or heard someone describe an annuity as being either a "qualified" or a "nonqualified" annuity. This aspect of "qualification" refers to whether the annuity is associated with a type of employee benefit plan (such as a pension fund or other type of retirement plan) that meets certain tax requirements contained in the U.S. Internal Revenue Code and in the Employee Retirement Income Security Act (ERISA).

Employer-sponsored retirement plans that satisfy the complex legal requirements of the Internal Revenue Code and ERISA and, as a result, provide certain favorable tax treatments for both the employer and employee are known as *tax-qualified plans*. *Qualified annuities* are purchased to fund or distribute funds from a tax-qualified plan and are exempt from current income taxation during the accumulation period. (We will discuss more about income taxation of annuities in Chapter 7.)

A person or a legal entity such as a trust or corporation can purchase a *nonqualified annuity,* a type of annuity that has few limitations on the amount that can be invested but that does not receive all of the tax advantages afforded qualified annuities.

Fixed and Variable Annuities

Annuities can also be categorized depending on how the annuity premiums are invested and what guarantees the annuity offers. Because of the significant differences between fixed and variable annuities, we will devote a chapter to each of these types of annuity contracts later in the text. However, at this point you will need to understand the characteristics that distinguish one from the other.

A *fixed annuity* is one for which the insurer guarantees to pay a specified rate of interest on the *accumulated value*—the net amount paid for the annuity plus interest earned, less the amount of any withdrawals or fees—for a specified period of time. As compared to a variable annuity, a fixed annuity provides more guarantees from the insurer to the contract owner, and consequently is viewed as a more conservative financial product.

Fixed annuity premiums are deposited in the insurer's *general account*, the general fund of assets invested to support the insurer's traditional insurance products.

A *variable annuity* is an annuity under which the amount of the contract's accumulated value and the amount of the periodic annuity payments fluctuate in accordance with the performance of a specified pool of investments. Variable annuity premiums are deposited in a *separate account*, an investment account maintained separately from an insurer's general account to help manage the funds placed in variable insurance products such as variable annuities. In Canada, the separate account is known as a *segregated account*. The insurer's separate account may include a number of *subaccounts*, investment funds that allow the insurer to place variable annuity premiums in a wide variety of investments. (Separate accounts and subaccounts will be discussed in Chapter 4.) Variable annuities generally offer no guarantees. The annuity premiums are invested in one or more subaccounts of a separate account, and the contract owner retains the risk associated with the subaccount investments.

Payout Period Options

Annuities can also be classified by the type of periodic payment option that the contract owner chooses. At this point, we will briefly describe the three most popular annuity payment options. We will discuss this topic in considerable detail in Chapter 2.

A *straight life annuity* provides periodic payments only for as long as the annuitant lives. Upon the death of the annuitant, the insurer has no further responsibility under the annuity contract. A *life income with period certain annuity* guarantees that annuity payments will be made throughout the annuitant's lifetime, but also guarantees that the payments will be made for at least a certain period, even if the annuitant dies before the end of that period. A *joint and survivor annuity* provides a series of periodic payments to more than one person, and those payments continue until the death of the last surviving annuitant.

From this brief overview of the types of annuities, we can see that annuities are complex products for consumers to understand. Despite their complexity, annuities have achieved considerable popularity in recent years. Two factors are contributing to this boom in annuity sales: (1) an aging population—many people are realizing that they may not have adequate retirement savings, and (2) a shift of responsibility for amassing retirement savings from employers to employees. In the current economic and social environment, financial services professionals have an opportunity to provide a valuable service to individuals who are interested in saving for retirement by educating them about the possibilities of annuities. Insight 1-1 discusses one study's view of the role of annuities as retirement savings vehicles.

Study Lauds Annuities as Savings Vehicles.

Annuities are likely to increase in importance as vehicles for financing retirement, according to a new study published by the Catalyst Institute. This Chicago-based think tank found that the most distinctive features of annuities—namely, the income options during the liquidation phase—help people manage cash flow, something that will become increasingly important in the future.

The study's authors predicted that "the average retirement period will probably continue to lengthen as a consequence of rising life expectancies and trends toward early retirement, thereby making prudent retirement cash-flow management all the more crucial." For that reason, they added, "public policy toward savings in general, and annuities in particular, should make meeting these emerging challenges as easy as possible for future retirees."

According to the study, annuities present powerful incentives to save from both the economic perspective and the behavioral perspective. Not only do annuities allow people to insure against the possibility of outliving their resources; they make dealing with the complexities of long-term financial planning easier for most people.

In addition, the study said, annuity contracts are often structured in ways that help people exercise self-control, because they are generally reluctant to invade dedicated retirement accounts for purposes other than retirement, and that reluctance is reinforced by penalties for early withdrawal. Similarly, the availability of payment plan options facilitates self-control after retirement by helping retirees manage cash flow.

The study concluded that the United States must actively change policies that hinder private savings and must take measures to stimulate thrift. According to the authors, "the situation requires a national campaign designed to reshape current social norms, combined with substantive, high-profile economic incentives. Annuities can play an important role in this process."

Source: Adapted from Steven Brostoff, "Study Lauds Annuities as Savings Vehicles," *National Underwriter* (April 6, 1998): 30. Used with permission.

KEY TERMS AND CONCEPTS

annuity
annuity contract
contract owner
annuitant
payee
beneficiary
non-natural owner
joint annuitant
immediate annuity
annuity period
deferred annuity
accumulation period
payout period
single-premium annuity
single-premium immediate annuity (SPIA)
single-premium deferred annuity (SPDA)
window premiums
flexible-premium annuity
tax-qualified plan
qualified annuity
nonqualified annuity
fixed annuity
accumulated value

general account
variable annuity
separate account
segregated account
subaccount
straight life annuity
life income with period certain annuity
joint and survivor annuity

CHAPTER 2

The Annuity Contract

After studying this chapter, you should be able to

◆ Describe the process involved in applying for an annuity contract

◆ Define terms found in an annuity contract that are important during the accumulation period

◆ Discuss the accumulation period of the annuity contract

◆ Define terms found in an annuity contract that are important during the payout period

◆ Discuss the payout period of the annuity contract

In the last chapter, we defined the key roles in the annuity contract—the insurer, the contract owner, the annuitant, the payee, and the beneficiary. In this chapter, we will discuss the role that the contract itself performs when annuities are purchased and issued. When they appear in annuity contracts, many of the contract provisions that we will discuss contain lengthy descriptions of administrative and procedural details. For the purposes of this chapter, we simply will provide the highlights of such contract provisions.

As we mentioned in Chapter 1, the annuity contract is a legally enforceable written agreement under which a person or an entity pays a premium or series of premiums to an insurer, and, in exchange, the insurer promises to make a series of periodic payments to a named person, starting on a specified date. Because the terms of the annuity contract govern the rights and duties of the contracting parties, you need to understand some of the most common provisions found in annuity contracts. Keep in mind that each insurance company will have a unique contract for each annuity product that it sells, and that each contract will have a unique set of provisions. Many of the provisions that we

discuss in this chapter are required by law in most states to be included in annuity contracts but may not be defined in exactly the same way that we define them here. In addition, the type of annuity being purchased—immediate, deferred, fixed, or variable—will also affect the provisions of the contract.

Because some provisions apply only at certain stages in the process, we have divided our discussion of annuity contracts into three parts: the application and contract process, the accumulation period, and the payout period. As we discuss these phases, we will consider contract provisions that typically are found in annuity contracts. If a particular provision applies only to a certain type of annuity, we will indicate that in the discussion.

THE PROCESS OF APPLYING FOR AN ANNUITY CONTRACT

As is true of anyone who enters into any contract, the person applying for the annuity contract must be competent to enter into a contract. And, just as a person who purchases life insurance or other type of insurance must provide certain information by completing an application or—in the case of a paperless application process—a reasonable facsimile, so must a person who purchases an annuity contract. Much of our discussion in the following section will refer to an application, but you should be aware that many insurance companies who sell annuities do not require the applicant to complete an application. The information provided by the applicant may be transmitted electronically to the insurer.

The applicant supplies information—such as the proposed annuitant's age and gender—that the insurer needs for determining the benefits to be provided by the annuity. During the application process, the applicant also receives information about the general characteristics and provisions of the annuity that he is purchasing.

Applicant Information

You'll recall from our discussion in Chapter 1 that many of the key provisions of an annuity contract require information about the contract owner and the annuitant. The current age of the annuitant is needed to calculate the length of the accumulation period—in the case of a deferred annuity—and to estimate the duration of payments for the payout period of some types of annuity contracts. Information on age is also needed because annuity contracts generally specify a maximum issue age for annuitants. The maximum issue age for an annuitant is typically between 70 and 85 years.

The annuity application requires the applicant to indicate the gender of the annuitant, because women have different life expectancies than men. When insurers estimate payments for an annuity contract, they use mortality tables to determine how long the annuitant is expected to live. Annuity mortality tables project both the death rate in a particular age group and the number of people who will survive each year—and thus receive annuity payments. Women generally live longer than men of the same age and are expected to receive payments from an annuity for a longer time period. In jurisdictions where paying different benefits because of gender is considered unlawfully discriminatory, however, insurers use unisex mortality tables. Even in states that require insurers to use unisex mortality tables, the applicant still might be asked to indicate the annuitant's gender on the application for identification purposes.

Contract Ownership

Usually, the applicant for an annuity contract is the contract owner. Although in most cases the contract owner and the annuitant are the same person, cases do occur where they are two different persons. Therefore, the applicant may also provide the contract owner's gender and age. (This information is not requested in the case of a group annuity where the contract owner is a legal entity, such as an employer.)

Ownership of an annuity contract can be shared with one or more additional persons. A *joint owner* actually shares ownership of the annuity contract. In some types of joint ownership, any decisions made about the contract would require the approval of both the contract owner and the joint owner.

And just as the contract owner can name the annuitant, she also may be able to name a *contingent annuitant*, a person who would become the annuitant if the primary annuitant were to die during the accumulation period of an annuity whose contract owner and annuitant are two different persons. As you will recall, the annuitant is the person whose lifetime is used to measure the length of time benefits are payable under the annuity contract.

Another important annuity contract provision related to contract ownership is the *assignment provision*, which grants the contract owner of a non-qualified annuity the ability to temporarily or permanently transfer ownership of the contract. For example, a contract owner might wish to use the cash value of an individual annuity as collateral for a loan by temporarily assigning the ownership rights to a bank during the loan repayment period. An assignment may have adverse tax consequences. (We will discuss the possible adverse tax implications of such an assignment in Chapter 7.) Some annuity contracts, however, do not allow assignment of the contract.

General Provisions of the Contract

Some general provisions that are found in life insurance contracts are also found in annuity contracts, although their form differs slightly. One such provision is the *entire contract provision,* which specifies that only those documents attached to or appearing in the contract are part of the contract. This provision is designed to protect both parties to a contract—in this case, the annuity contract owner and the insurer. The entire contract provision protects the contract owner by ensuring that she will have a written copy of all the rules governing her annuity contract, because those rules are contained in her copy of the contract. No part of the contract can be modified after issue without the contract owner's consent. The entire contract provision also stipulates that changes to the contract can only be made in writing by a designated officer of the insurance company and may include a sentence that says any oral statements made by any party to the contract are not part of the contract. In other words, if something is not in writing, it's not part of the contract.

The annuity contract also contains an *incontestability provision*, which states that after the contract becomes effective, the insurer generally cannot contest it. This provision is much more restrictive to the insurer than its counterpart in life insurance policies. Contracts that include certain waivers, however, may have different incontestability provisions.

Unlike a life insurance application that asks for information regarding the applicant's insurability—information that the applicant may misstate—an annuity application typically does not request information about the applicant's insurability. So, although a life insurance policy may allow the insurer as long as two years after policy issue to contest a policy because of misstatements made by the applicant, an annuity contract generally does not need such a provision. Even in the case of a misstatement of the age or sex of an annuitant, many annuity contracts stipulate that if the annuitant's age or sex is misstated, the insurer will pay annuity benefits based on the correct age or sex.

An exception to the rule that incontestability provisions do not allow the insurer to contest an annuity contract would be in the case of an annuity contract that includes a *waiver of premium for disability rider*, a provision that allows the contract owner to stop making premium payments in the event that he becomes disabled. To obtain a waiver of premium for disability rider, the applicant is required to provide proof of insurability. Therefore, an incontestability provision like those found in life insurance policies then becomes a part of this annuity contract, thus allowing the insurer to contest the contract because of misstatements during the first two years after the annuity is issued.

The rule of thumb is, if an annuity contract does not require proof of insurability, the incontestability clause states that the insurer cannot contest the contract once it has become effective. However, if the annuity contract contains a rider that requires the applicant to submit proof of insurability, then the annuity contract will contain an incontestability clause allowing the insurer to contest the contract—usually for a period of two years—for misstatements made in the application.

Individual deferred fixed annuity contracts must also contain a *nonforfeiture provision*, which states that if the contract owner stops making premium payments, he will still receive an annuity benefit based on the amount of premiums he has paid. The nonforfeiture provision also states that if the annuity contract provides for settlement in a lump sum, the contract must provide that, on surrender of the contract during the accumulation period, the insurer will pay a lump sum to the contract owner in lieu of an annuity benefit.

Purchase Payments

The initial payment for an annuity may accompany the application. For an immediate annuity or for any single-premium annuity, the initial payment is the only payment. If the annuity being purchased provides for multiple premium payments, then the application may specify how frequently the contract owner will make subsequent payments—monthly, quarterly, semiannually, or annually—or that no subsequent payments are *required*, although they are permitted. The application may also stipulate how those payments will be made—for example, by automatic deposit.

In the case of a fixed annuity, which pays a guaranteed rate of interest for a specified time period or contract duration, the applicant will also choose the contract duration. At the end of the specified period, the insurer will determine the interest rate that will be paid for the next period. Most fixed annuities will guarantee a higher interest rate than usual if the applicant accepts that rate for a longer period of time. We will discuss how insurers determine and guarantee interest rates on fixed annuities in much greater detail in Chapter 3.

If the applicant is purchasing a variable annuity, the application will require the contract owner to choose the subaccounts where he wants his premiums to be deposited. He will indicate how he wishes his initial payment to be distributed among the insurer's subaccounts, as well as how he wishes future payments to be credited. We provide a much more detailed discussion of variable annuity subaccounts in Chapter 4.

Free Look Provision

To protect consumers, state laws require many types of contracts to include a provision that allows the consumer to change his mind about entering into the contract. Insurers have incorporated such a provision into annuity contracts. The *free look provision* states that the contract owner has a period of time—usually 10 to 20 days—to examine the annuity contract, with the option of returning it to the insurer during this time for a full refund of the premium paid. In some states, if the contract owner returns a variable annuity contract under the free look provision, the insurer refunds the current market value of the contract.

THE ACCUMULATION PERIOD

As we noted in Chapter 1, the time period between the date that the contract owner purchases the annuity and the date that the payee begins to receive payments is known as the accumulation period. Because payments for immediate annuities begin within one annuity period of the purchase of the annuity contract, immediate annuities have no accumulation period. However, deferred annuities, even single-premium deferred annuities, are left on deposit for a period of time. During this accumulation period, numerous provisions govern the operation of the annuity contract.

Premium Payments

If the annuity contract establishes a flexible-premium deferred annuity, premium payments may continue throughout the accumulation period. In the next section, we will discuss premium payments to a fixed annuity and premium payments to a variable annuity.

Premium Payments to a Fixed Annuity

In Chapter 1, we discussed the various methods by which contract owners can make premium payments. The most important factor that affects fixed annuity premium payments is the guarantee regarding the interest rate that will be credited to those payments.

With a fixed annuity, the insurance company specifies a ***guaranteed interest rate***—typically 3 or 4 percent—that it will pay on the annuity's balance for the duration of the annuity contract. In addition, for some types of fixed annuity contracts, when the contract is purchased, the insurer also promises to pay the ***current interest rate***—one that is based on the interest rates prevailing in the economy—for a specified time period, usually for one, three, or five years. When the specified period ends, the insurer declares a new interest rate—the ***renewal rate***—for a subsequent period. The renewal rate may be higher or lower than the current interest rate, depending upon conditions in the general economy and how the insurer has invested the funds. The insurer will offer various current interest rates depending on the time period that the contract owner desires. Generally, the contract owner may choose the duration of the current interest rate on his contract from a number of options. See Figure 2-1 for an example of current interest rates on annuity products with corresponding time commitments—actual rates depend on general economic conditions and the investment practices of the insurer.

FIGURE 2.1

Sample Current Interest Rates for a Fixed Annuity.

Interest Rate	Interest Rate	Interest Rate
5.85%	**5.50%**	**5.00%**
5 year	**3** year	**1** year
guarantee	guarantee	guarantee

As we have stated, in addition to the current interest rate that the insurer promises to pay during each time period, the insurer generally guarantees that a fixed annuity's interest rate will not fall below a stated minimum rate such as 3.0 or 4.0 percent. For example, suppose Rose Harker purchases a fixed annuity with a three-year guarantee on a current interest rate of 5.5 percent and a guaranteed interest rate of 3.0 percent. If, at the end of the three-year period, the renewal rate were 5.0 percent, Ms. Harker's annuity would earn 5.0 percent for the next three-year period. In the unlikely event that the insurer's investment earnings fall below 3.0 percent at some time in the future, the insurer would still be obligated to pay 3.0 percent interest on Ms. Harker's annuity contract, even though the insurer would not be earning that rate on its investments.

Premium Payments to a Variable Annuity

The owner of a variable annuity invests premium payments in an insurer's separate account by purchasing **accumulation units**, which represent ownership shares in selected subaccounts of the separate account. Each subaccount represents a different type of investment with its own investment objective and rate of return potential. Rates of return for these accounts are not guaranteed. We will discuss variable annuity subaccounts in greater detail in Chapter 4.

Another important contract provision that affects variable annuity premium payments involves ensuring the consistent distribution of premium payments among the subaccounts as specified by the contract owner on the application. For example, a contract owner may want to divide the premiums and the accumulated balance evenly between two separate subaccounts. If the value of one of those accounts changes dramatically, the balances of the two accounts may no longer be equal. Many insurers have a contract provision known as the **automatic rebalancing provision**, which states that values automatically will be transferred between specified accounts to maintain the allocation percentages designated by the contract owner. In Chapter 4, the process for automatic rebalancing will be discussed further.

Insurance Company Fees/Charges

The annuity contract also outlines the various administrative fees and charges the insurer will charge the contract owner. The fees charged depend on the type of annuity and the insurance company that issues the annuity. In the following section, we discuss some of the fees that are typically charged in conjunction with different types of annuities.

Administrative Fees

The insurer may charge a set **administrative fee** for variable or fixed annuities to cover costs such as issuing the annuity, making administrative changes to the annuity contract, and preparing the contract owner's statement. Generally, the more "maintenance" that an annuity requires on the part of the insurer, the more likely that some type of administrative fee will be charged. In the case of some fixed annuity contracts, such fees are not charged separately but have been included in the premiums charged for the contract. Variable annuities may have separate annual administrative fees that typically range from $25 to $50. However, some insurers only charge an administrative fee for a variable annuity contract whose value is below a certain amount—$25,000, for example—on the contract anniversary date.

Surrender Charges

Insurance companies may impose a penalty known as a **surrender charge** for withdrawing funds from an annuity. This surrender charge is calculated as a percentage of the annuity contract value withdrawn on the date of the withdrawal and may decrease over time. An insurer typically imposes surrender charges during the early years of an annuity policy in order to recoup the costs it incurred in issuing the policy and to discourage early withdrawal. Figure 2-2 shows a sample of a typical surrender charge schedule.

FIGURE 2.2

Surrender Charge Schedule.

Contract Year	Surrender Charge (Percentage of withdrawal)
1	7.0%
2	6.0%
3	5.0%
4	4.0%
5	3.0%
6	2.0%
7	1.0%
8 and thereafter	0.0%

In most cases, after the contract owner has owned the annuity for a certain number of years, surrender charges do not apply. In some cases, these charges are associated with the date on which premiums were deposited into the account or are based on the amount of money in the annuity and not on the contract year.

Fees on Variable Annuities

As we discussed in Chapter 1, premiums for variable annuities are invested in one or more investment funds via the subaccounts in the insurer's separate account. Variable annuities charge an **asset management fee** to cover the management costs and operating expenses associated with the underlying investment funds.

Variable annuity contracts also include a **mortality and expense risks (M&E) charge**, which is a fee that provides for payment of a death benefit, ensures that the expense risks charged on the contract won't increase, and also covers a guaranteed interest rate that is paid on one type of variable annuity subaccount. This charge also covers overhead expenses the insurer incurs with respect to the annuity contract. A typical M&E charge ranges from 1.00 to 1.75 percent of the contract value.

Withdrawals

As we will stress throughout this text, the intended purpose of annuities is to fund retirement. Because the federal government wants to encourage people to save for retirement, both individual and group annuities have numerous tax advantages, a topic that we will discuss extensively in Chapter 7. However, because of these tax advantages, a withdrawal by a contract owner from an annuity prior to the age of 59½ usually will carry a federal tax penalty and may cause the contract owner to incur federal taxes due on contributions or accumulations that previously have not been taxed. As we have already noted, the insurer also may assess a surrender charge on withdrawals prior to retirement.

However, insurers know that many potential annuity purchasers are reluctant to tie up funds they might need in case of an emergency. Therefore, annuity contracts typically include a *free withdrawal provision*, which grants the contract owner the right to withdraw all or a portion of the annuity's accumulated value during the accumulation period. Many annuities allow for withdrawals of between 10 and 15 percent of the annuity's value per year without a surrender charge.

Some annuity products permit unused free withdrawals to accumulate so that if the contract owner does not take a withdrawal in one year, she may take the unused amount in the following year. If the contract owner withdraws more than the free withdrawal amount in one year, then the insurer generally imposes a surrender charge, as we discussed earlier. Withdrawals of less than a stated minimum amount typically are not permitted. Of course, the contract owner would be required to pay any taxes or tax penalties on these withdrawals.

Surrender Provision

Throughout a deferred annuity's accumulation period a contract owner can also make a type of withdrawal known as a *surrender*, which involves withdrawing the annuity contract's entire accumulated value less any surrender charges included in the policy—the *cash surrender value*. A surrender charge is typically imposed if the policy is surrendered within a stated number of years after it was purchased, and the amount of the charge may decline over time.

If the contract owner surrenders an annuity, the annuity contract ends before the annuity becomes due and no annuity payments are made. As is true in the case of partial withdrawals, the contract owner would be required to pay any taxes or tax penalties on the cash surrender. A sample surrender provision is shown in Figure 2-3.

Many annuity contracts also include a *waiver of surrender charge provision*, which states that the insurer will not subject a withdrawal to a surrender charge under certain specified conditions. The most common

---

FIGURE 2.3

Sample Surrender Provision.

At or before the commencement of any annuity payment, all or part of the contract's value may be withdrawn on request of the Contract Owner. The amount of cash paid on a surrender will be the accumulated value withdrawn, less any surrender charge on such value.

Partial withdrawals may be subject to one or more of the following conditions:

1. Only one partial withdrawal may be made in a policy year.
2. A partial withdrawal may not be for less than $1,000.
3. A partial withdrawal may not be made if the remaining accumulated value would be less than $5,000.

The surrender charge may be deducted from any withdrawal made during the first policy year. On the first partial withdrawal made during any subsequent policy year, no surrender charge will be deducted from any amount withdrawn that is less than or equal to 10% of the accumulated value on the date of the withdrawal. However, if all of the accumulated value is withdrawn, appropriate surrender charges will be deducted from the full amount withdrawn.

---

circumstances under which the insurer will waive surrender charges include the disability or poor medical condition of the contract owner, terminal illness of the contract owner, unemployment of the contract owner, and confinement of the contract owner in a nursing home or hospital. Surrender charges also are waived if a contract owner elects to begin receiving annuity payments.

Bailout Provision

One feature that affords annuity contract owners a certain degree of protection from surrender charges is the bailout provision. A **bailout provision** (sometimes known as an *escape clause* or *cash-out provision*) enables the contract owner to surrender the annuity contract, usually without a surrender charge, if renewal interest rates on a fixed annuity fall below a pre-established level, typically 1 percent below the initial interest rate. However, the contract owner may have to pay taxes on the amount surrendered, as well as a 10 percent tax penalty if she is younger than 59½ years old.

Loans on Qualified Annuities

Although most nonqualified individual annuity contracts do not allow the contract owner to obtain a loan against the annuity balance, many qualified annuities, which establish individual accounts for each employee, do include a contract provision that allows the contract owner to obtain a loan. Strictly speaking, these loans are not withdrawals, because the contract owner must repay his own account with interest. An important distinction exists between a loan and a withdrawal. A loan is guaranteed by the cash value in the annuity, so the cash value securing the loan is not available to the contract owner until the loan is repaid. In contrast to a loan, a withdrawal is a permanent reduction. In addition, loans and withdrawals are treated differently for tax purposes.

Death Benefit Provisions

Many annuity contracts include provisions that describe how annuity benefits will be paid upon the death of the contract owner or the annuitant. If the contract owner dies during the accumulation period, the insurer will pay to the beneficiary the value of the annuity account as of the date the insurer receives the proof of death. If the annuitant dies during the payout period, the insurer may continue to make the remaining annuity payments depending upon the type of payout option specified in the annuity contract.

Although variable annuities do not provide guarantees with regard to interest rates or safety of principal, they usually include a minimum death benefit. The **death benefit guarantee** states that if the contract owner dies before the annuity payments begin, the beneficiary named by the contract owner will receive a benefit equal to the greater of (1) the total amount of premium payments made for the annuity, less any withdrawals made, or (2) the accumulated value at the time of the contract owner's death. The death benefit guarantee ensures that the beneficiary will receive at least the amount that was deposited into the variable annuity contract, less any withdrawals, even if poor investment performance causes the accumulated value of the contract to be less than the premiums paid. However, if the accumulated value at the time of the contract owner's death is greater than the premiums paid because subaccount investments have performed well, the beneficiary will receive the accumulated value.

THE PAYOUT PERIOD

As you recall, the period during which annuity payments are made is known as the payout period. As we have also pointed out, the payout period for a single-premium immediate annuity (SPIA) begins one annuity period after the date on which the annuity is purchased, and the payout period for a deferred annuity begins more than one annuity period after the annuity is purchased. When a deferred annuity's accumulation period ends and the payout period begins, the annuity is said to *mature* or *annuitize*. The date on which the insurer begins to make annuity payments is often called the annuity's **income date**, also known as the *maturity date* or the *annuity date*.

When an annuity matures, the insurer uses the money that has accumulated in the annuity to fund the periodic annuity payments. In an annuity contract, the **payout option provision**, also known as the *settlement option provision*, lists and describes each of the payout options from which the contract owner may select. In the case of an immediate annuity, the applicant chooses the payout option when he applies for the annuity. However, in the case of a deferred annuity, the contract owner chooses the payout option just prior to the beginning of the payout period. Choosing the correct option for a person's unique circumstances is a complex process, particularly when one considers the tax implications for different payouts, a topic that we will explore further in Chapter 7. In this section, we will describe some of the payout options available in an annuity contract. You will recall that, in most cases, the contract owner, the annuitant, and the payee are all the same person. However, as was the case in our discussion in Chapter 1, in the following discussion, the contract owner is the person who makes all decisions, including choosing the payout option; the annuitant is the person whose life expectancy determines the amount and duration of payments; and the payee receives the annuity payments.

Lump Sum Distribution

Some contract owners choose to receive the balance of their accounts in a single payment known as a *lump sum distribution*. The reason for choosing a lump sum distribution may be to fund the purchase of a retirement home or to pay for an extended trip. However, the taxes incurred on a lump sum distribution can reduce the distribution significantly. Some contract owners may have the option of averaging the income from a lump sum distribution over several years.

Fixed Period or Fixed Amount

Under the *fixed period* option, the insurer makes annuity payments for a specified period of time. With the *fixed amount* option, the insurer determines the length of time that the annuity's accumulated value will provide a preselected periodic payment.

With both the fixed period option and the fixed amount option, the amount of time that the annuitant lives does not affect the duration or the amount of payments, because the payee or a *contingent payee*—a person designated by the contract owner to receive payments upon the death of the payee—will receive the entire balance of the account. An annuity that is payable for a stated period of time, regardless of whether the annuitant lives or dies, is called an *annuity certain*. The stated period over which the insurer will make the payments is called the *period certain*. At the end of the period certain, annuity payments cease, because all of the accumulated value of the annuity contract will have been distributed either to the payee or to the contingent payee.

Annuitization

The payout options described so far do not make use of one of the primary features of an annuity—to provide an income that cannot be outlived. In fact, despite this powerful advantage of annuities, many contract owners do not choose a payout option that provides payments throughout the annuitant's lifetime. Insurers have recently begun to address this issue by stressing to their contract owners the value of *annuitization*, a payout option that involves payments tied to a life expectancy.

Straight Life Annuity

A *life annuity* is an annuity that provides periodic payments for at least the lifetime of the annuitant. Some life annuities, described below, also provide further payment guarantees. You'll recall from our discussion in Chapter 1 that a straight life annuity provides periodic payments only for as long as the annuitant lives. Upon the death of the annuitant, the insurer makes no further payments. Because of the uncertainty of when an annuitant will die, the contract owner who chooses a straight life annuity runs the risk that she may pay a great deal more in premiums than the payee will receive in annuity payments. Many people are unwilling to accept such a risk, and, therefore, they purchase annuities that contain more guarantees than are contained in a straight life annuity. Of course, it is also true that the annuitant whose life expectancy is used to calculate the payments made under a straight life annuity may live well beyond the average life expectancy and the payee will receive a great deal more in annuity payments than the contract owner paid in to the contract.

Life Income with Period Certain Annuity

As we mentioned in Chapter 1, a life income with period certain annuity guarantees that annuity payments will be made throughout the annuitant's lifetime. Payments will continue to be made for at least a certain period, even if the annuitant dies before the end of that period. The contract owner selects the guaranteed period, which can be 5, 10, 15, or 20 years. Typically, for annuities that are similar in all other particulars, the longer the guaranteed period, the smaller the amount of each annuity payment.

In addition to choosing the guaranteed period, the contract owner names a contingent payee. If the payee dies before the period certain has expired, then the contingent payee receives the periodic payments throughout the remainder of the period certain. If the annuitant is living when the period certain expires, the payee continues to receive payments for the rest of the annuitant's life. In such a case, annuity payments end with the annuitant's death.

Life Income with Refund Annuity

The *life income with refund annuity*, also known as a *refund annuity*, provides annuity payments throughout the lifetime of the annuitant and guarantees that at least the purchase price of the annuity will be paid out. This guarantee means that if the annuitant dies before the total of the payments made equals the purchase price, a refund will be made. The amount of the refund, which can be paid in a lump sum or in installments, is equal to the difference between the purchase price of the annuity and the amount that has been paid out.

Joint and Survivor Annuity

The settlement options that we have discussed so far have involved situations in which a life annuity was based on the life expectancy of one annuitant. You'll recall that a life annuity, however, can provide an income based upon the life expectancy of more than one person. Usually this type of annuity is used to provide payments that will continue throughout the lives of two people. As we discussed in Chapter 1, a joint and survivor annuity provides a series of periodic payments based upon the life expectancy of two or more annuitants, and those payments continue until all the annuitants die.

The terms of a joint and survivor annuity contract determine whether the amount of each periodic annuity payment remains the same after the death of one of the annuitants. For example, the annuity contract might provide that the amount of the periodic payment will remain the same until the last annuitant dies, or the annuity might provide that the amount of the periodic payment will be reduced by a stated amount, such as 50 percent, following the death of the first annuitant. Of course, the premium amount required to fund the annuity will vary, depending upon the ages and gender of the annuitants and the amounts that are to be paid out. The larger the expected amount of payments, the larger the premium required to pay for the annuity.

Fixed and Variable Payout Options

The owner of a fixed annuity will receive a *fixed payout*, which means that annuity payments remain the same during the payout period. The owner of a variable contract can also choose a fixed payout option and receive a guaranteed payment amount. Or, the owner of a variable annuity may choose a *variable payout*, which means that the payments are not fixed but vary based on the performance of the underlying subaccounts. This option is somewhat more complex than the fixed payout option. The choice of variable payout entails a degree of risk for the contract owner that does not exist in the fixed payout option, but the variable payout option also offers the potential that payments will increase over time, allowing the payee's income to keep pace with inflation. A variable contract owner also has the option of receiving a combination of fixed and variable payouts. Figure 2-4 summarizes the various annuity payout options.

Calculating the Annuity Payment

Four variables that influence the size of an annuity's periodic payment are

- ◆ The amount of premiums paid into the annuity
- ◆ The time over which the principal accumulates
- ◆ The interest rate or investment returns
- ◆ The number of periodic annuity payments

Actual annuity contract calculations are beyond the scope of this text, but Figure 2-5 summarizes the effect that changing one of the variables generally has on the periodic payment from a fixed annuity.

FIGURE 2.4   **Annuity Payout Options.**

Payout Option	Payout Type	Payout Length
Fixed Period	Fixed	Equal to total accumulated contract value for a specified period of time. Payment amount determined by time.
Fixed Amount	Fixed	Equal to total accumulated contract value at a specified payment for a specified period of time. Time determined by amount of payment.
Straight Life	Variable or Fixed	Annuitant's lifetime.
Life Income with Period Certain	Variable or Fixed	Annuitant's lifetime with guarantee that payments will continue for a specified minimum period, if annuitant dies during guaranteed period.
Life Income with Refund	Variable or Fixed	Lifetime of annuitant with guarantee that payments continue after annuitant's death until annuity purchase price or the accumulated value of the contract has been paid out.
Joint and Survivor	Variable or Fixed	Lifetime of two or more annuitants.

FIGURE 2.5   **Effect of Changing Variables on the Size of Periodic Payments in a Fixed Annuity Equation.**

Variable	If you...	Then the size of the periodic payments will...
Amount of Premiums Paid	↑ **Increase** the amount of premiums	↑ **Increase**, because the account value will be larger.
	↓ **Decrease** the amount of premiums	↓ **Decrease**, because the account value will be smaller.
Accumulation Period	↑ **Increase** the accumulation period	↑ **Increase**, because the account value will have more time to accumulate interest.
	↓ **Decrease** the accumulation period	↓ **Decrease**, because the account value will have a shorter time in which to accumulate interest.
Stated Interest Rate	↑ **Increase** the stated interest rate	↑ **Increase**, because the account value will earn a higher interest rate.
	↓ **Decrease** the stated interest rate	↓ **Decrease**, because the account value will earn a lower interest rate, which in turn will decrease earnings.
Number of Periodic Payments	↑ **Increase** the number of periodic payments in the series of payments	↓ **Decrease**, because you will have to spread the same amount of money over a larger number of payments.
	↓ **Decrease** the number of periodic payments	↑ **Increase**, because you will have a smaller number of payments over which to spread the accumulated principal and interest.

Insight 2-1 illustrates how some of the contract provisions we have discussed influence the operation of a fixed annuity contract.

Appendix A includes a sample annuity contract to illustrate what an annuity contract looks like. Because insurers use different terminology for the same terms and provisions, some of the terms in the sample are not the same as the ones we have used in the text discussion. Also, not all provisions discussed in the text are used in the sample contract.

INSIGHT 2.1

A Fixed Annuity Purchase and Payout.

When he was 48 years old, Henry Lee inherited $50,000, which he used to purchase a single-premium deferred annuity that earns an annual return of 6 percent. Under the terms of the annuity contract, Mr. Lee will begin receiving monthly periodic annuity payments starting the month of his 65th birthday, continuing for the rest of his life.

The four variables affecting Mr. Lee's annuity contract are (1) $50,000, the premium Mr. Lee paid into the annuity; (2) 17 years (65–48), the time over which the principal will accumulate at interest; (3) 6 percent, the interest rate; and (4) payments for life, the number of periodic annuity payments. If one of the four variables changes, the result of the mathematical calculation changes.

For example, increasing the amount that Mr. Lee used to purchase the annuity would result in an increase in the amount of the periodic annuity payment. If Mr. Lee had purchased a $60,000 annuity, the periodic payments would have been larger than the payments for the $50,000 annuity, everything else being equal.

Similarly, changes in the interest rate that the fixed annuity earns would also change the result of the calculation. If the interest rate earned by the annuity increases, the amount of the periodic annuity payment will increase—the higher the interest rate, the larger the amount of interest income the annuity will earn. And, the more income that is earned, the larger will be the total amount of money available to fund the periodic annuity payments. Therefore, an annual return of 7 percent would provide a larger periodic payment than a return of 6 percent.

Let's assume, for purposes of comparing annuity options, that Mr. Lee decides when he purchases his annuity to wait until he is age 70 (instead of 65) to begin receiving monthly annuity payments. In this case, each monthly payment he receives will be larger than the monthly payments he would have received if he had begun payments at age 65. The payments would be larger for two reasons: (1) the initial $50,000 would have had five more years to earn interest and (2) at age 70, the period over which the insurer will make payments would presumably be shorter, since the period between age 70 and Mr. Lee's eventual death is shorter than the period between age 65 and his eventual death.

To compare a period certain option to a life income option, we would have to make certain assumptions about Mr. Lee's life expectancy. Let's imagine that when Mr. Lee buys the annuity, the life expectancy for male annuitants age 65 (the age he wants to begin receiving payments) is 15 years. If he had chosen to begin receiving monthly payments at age 65 for a set period of 10 years instead of for life, the amount of each monthly payment would be larger. Under the 10-year period certain option, the insurer knows it will make payments for exactly 10 years, which is a shorter time period than the period the insurer used in its assumptions about the life income option.

Under the life income option, the insurer would have calculated the payment amount based on the probability that payments would be made to Mr. Lee for 15 years. Neither the insurance company nor Mr. Lee, of course, knows how long Mr. Lee will actually live. He could live to age 90, in which case the somewhat smaller payments made under the life income option would be made from age 65 to his death at age 90. That would turn out to be quite a bargain for him.

KEY TERMS AND CONCEPTS

joint owner
contingent annuitant
assignment provision
entire contract provision
incontestability provision

waiver of premium for disability rider
nonforfeiture provision
free look provision
guaranteed interest rate
current interest rate
renewal rate
accumulation units
automatic rebalancing provision
administrative fee
surrender charge
asset management fee
mortality and expense risks (M&E) charge
free withdrawal provision
surrender
cash surrender value
waiver of surrender charge provision
bailout provision
death benefit guarantee
income date
payout option provision
lump sum distribution
fixed period
fixed amount
contingent payee
annuity certain
period certain
annuitization
life annuity
life income with refund annuity
fixed payout
variable payout

CHAPTER 3

Fixed and Equity-Indexed Annuities

After studying this chapter, you should be able to

◆ Describe the characteristics of a fixed annuity

◆ Discuss the types of guarantees that a fixed annuity offers

◆ Explain the purpose of the insurer's general account

◆ Describe the characteristics of an equity-indexed annuity

◆ Discuss the types of guarantees that an equity-indexed annuity offers

In Chapter 1, we mentioned that annuities can be categorized by the way the funds are invested and the guarantees associated with the annuity. Our discussion defined a fixed annuity as one for which the insurer guarantees to pay a specified rate of interest on the annuity account value for a specified period of time. In addition to the traditional fixed annuity, a second type of fixed annuity is the equity-indexed annuity. An *equity-indexed annuity* offers the same type of interest rate guarantees as a traditional fixed annuity, but also may credit additional interest depending upon the performance of the stock market. In this chapter, we will explore the characteristics and features of fixed annuities and equity-indexed annuities.

FIXED ANNUITIES

The operation of a fixed annuity is fairly straightforward. Whether the contract owner purchases a fixed annuity with a single payment or a series of payments, the insurer will credit payments at the time of receipt with the current interest rate published by the insurer. You will recall from our discussion in Chapter 2 that the fixed annuity contract also specifies a guaranteed minimum interest rate—usually 3 to 4 percent—which sets a level that the interest credited cannot fall below.

The General Account

The insurer deposits fixed annuity premiums in a general account. As we mentioned in Chapter 1, an insurance company's investments consist of assets held in the insurer's general account and assets held in separate accounts. You'll recall that the insurer's general account is the general fund of assets invested to support the insurer's traditional insurance products.

An insurer must comply with numerous state laws in choosing investments for its general account. These laws are designed to ensure the safety of the assets in the general account. Therefore, depositing annuity premiums in the general account provides an element of security for contract owners who choose to purchase fixed annuities.

Interest Rate Guarantees

The insurer guarantees that, in most cases, owners of fixed annuity contracts will not lose the *principal*—the total amount invested in the annuity, exclusive of any investment returns—and that they will earn a certain interest rate on that money. Therefore, the insurer assumes all the investment risk associated with the product. If the investments in the general account perform well, the insurer can pay the interest rates guaranteed in its fixed annuity contracts while still achieving profits. However, even if the insurer's investments perform poorly and its investment returns are less than the minimums guaranteed in its contracts, the insurer still must pay the contract owner at least the guaranteed minimum interest rate stated in the annuity contract. The contract owner bears none of the investment risk.

Payout Guarantees

Besides guaranteeing the safety of the principal and the interest rate that will be paid, a fixed annuity contract also guarantees a minimum monthly annuity payment for each dollar of premium used to purchase the fixed annuity. Most fixed annuities specify that when the insurer begins making annuity payments, the amount of each payment will not change. A few fixed annuities, however, provide that payments may increase in direct relation to the interest rate credited. If current interest rates in the marketplace exceed those at the time when the insurer originally calculated the payment amount, the insurer may credit the annuity with the higher interest rate and increase the payments.

If the fixed annuity is an immediate annuity, then the contract owner and the insurer know the amount of each annuity payment when the insurer issues the annuity contract. The purchaser pays a single premium, and the insurer calculates the amount of each annuity payment that will be provided by that single premium.

If the fixed annuity is a deferred annuity, then the annuity contract includes a chart of annuity values, similar to the one shown in Figure 3-1.

FIGURE 3.1

Chart of Annuity Values for a Deferred Fixed Annuity.

Annuitant's Age	Payments for Life Only	Minimum Monthly Payments for Each $1,000 Applied		
		Payments Guaranteed for		
		10 Years	15 Years	20 Years
40	$4.13	$4.12	$4.11	$4.09
45	4.36	4.34	4.32	4.28
50	4.65	4.62	4.58	4.52
55	5.05	4.99	4.91	4.81
60	5.56	5.45	5.32	5.14
65	6.27	6.07	5.82	5.48
70	7.33	6.89	6.38	5.76
75 & over	8.95	7.89	6.87	5.92

This chart lists the amount that is guaranteed for each $1,000 of accumulated value. For example, according to the chart, if the annuity's accumulated value on the income date is $20,000 when the annuitant is age 40, the payment for life for each $1,000 is $4.13. So, the insurer will pay $82.60 per month (20 × $4.13 = $82.60) for the remainder of the annuitant's life. Note, however, that the amounts listed in the contract are the minimum guaranteed amounts that the insurer guaranteed when it issued the fixed annuity. If the insurer's investment experience is more favorable than expected, or current market conditions dictate paying a higher interest rate, then the insurer may pay more than the guaranteed amount.

Inflation Erosion

Although a fixed annuity does have the advantages of safety and a guaranteed return, one disadvantage of a fixed annuity is the potential loss of purchasing power in times of inflation. Monthly payments remain the same even if the recipient's monthly living expenses increase because of inflation. However, many contract owners or annuitants are willing to risk a loss of purchasing power to obtain the safety from investment risk offered by a fixed annuity. Insight 3-1 discusses why the guarantees offered by fixed annuities still appeal to some consumers.

INSIGHT 3.1   **Reevaluating What Is Important to Buyers.**

From time to time, it is a good idea to reevaluate what is important to annuity buyers. We know that safety is important and we know that tax deferral is important. Additionally, we know liquidity and income are important, as well as the death benefit. While it seems that all of these things are not connected, there is a consistent thread running through most of them. The thread of consistency is guarantees.

Guarantees are now, and always have been, very important to the buyers of annuities. There is no question today that a large part of the popularity of equity-indexed annuities is due to the guarantee of principal return (plus some interest) at term end, as well as the guarantee of interest, indexed to influences outside the carrier's control.

Regarding nonequity-indexed fixed annuities, guarantees continue to be as important as ever. As you know, these declared-rate fixed annuities are not hot sellers in a low interest rate environment; however, some clearly still sell. One reason declared-rate fixed annuities sell is due to their guarantees. The better selling products tend to be those with longer initial interest rate guarantees, even when those guaranteed rates are not very high.

Source: Adapted from Thomas F. Streiff, "Reevaluating What Is Important to Buyers," *National Underwriter* (January 5, 1998): 18. Used with permission.

EQUITY-INDEXED ANNUITIES

Although experts disagree about the nature of equity-indexed annuities, most agree that this type of annuity product most closely resembles a fixed annuity. The combination of a guaranteed interest rate and the possibility of additional earnings linked to the performance of the stock market has been very appealing to many customers.

The Index

Insurers design their equity-indexed annuities by linking the interest credited to the contract to a published *index*, a statistical measurement system that tracks the performance of a group of similar investments. Although no one can directly invest in an index, insurers can use a portion of equity-indexed annuity premiums to purchase investments whose performance is closely tied to the performance of a well-known and respected index, such as the Standard and Poor's Composite Stock Price Index, the S&P Midcap, or the Russell 2000.

Interest Rate Guarantees

Equity-indexed annuity contracts generally guarantee that the contract value will not fall below 90 percent of the invested money and will earn a certain interest rate on that money. One way in which equity-indexed annuities are similar to traditional fixed annuities is in the fact that premiums are deposited in the insurer's general account. These characteristics clearly differentiate equity-indexed annuities from variable annuities, which have no such guarantees and whose premiums are deposited in the insurer's separate account. We will discuss variable annuities in more detail in Chapter 4.

Calculating Excess Interest

In order for the insurer to pay out excess interest, the **term,** which is the length of time over which the interest will be calculated, must be specified in the equity-indexed annuity contract. Most equity-indexed annuities have terms that range from one year to ten years. The length of the term is critical—in many cases, the contract owner must hold the contract until the end of the term to receive the full value of the annuity, including excess interest credits.

The insurer can calculate the excess interest applied to an equity-indexed annuity in different ways. The individual annuity contract will specify which method is used to calculate excess credits. Most insurers use one of three different methods:

- ◆ Annual reset method
- ◆ High water mark method
- ◆ Point-to-point method

The **annual reset method,** also known as the *ratchet method,* involves comparing the value of the index at the start of the contract year with its value at the end of the contract year. The new starting value for the next year is reset to the value of the index at the end of the contract year. At the beginning of each contract year during the term of the contract, the value is reset. The insurer determines the amount of any index-based excess interest credit by averaging the results of each contract year of the contract term.

The **high water mark method** for calculating excess interest involves comparing the value of the index at the beginning of the term of the contract with the highest value that the index reaches at certain points, usually contract anniversary dates, during the term. If the index has gained in value on an anniversary date, the contract will be credited with excess interest for that year. However, if on a contract anniversary date, the index has remained the same or lost value compared to the index value at the start of the contract term, the contract will not be credited with excess interest for that year. In other words, the equity-indexed contract owner would share in upward movement of the index, while being protected against any downward movement.

The *point-to-point method* of calculating excess interest compares the value of the index at the start of the annuity contract term to its value at the end of the term to determine what, if any, excess interest has accrued because of a change in the index.

Crediting Excess Interest

Several contract provisions determine how much excess interest the insurer will credit to the equity-indexed annuity contract. Most equity-indexed annuities include each of the following provisions.

Many insurers specify a *participation rate*, which is the percentage of the specified index's gain in value that will be credited to the equity-indexed annuity contract. Insurers offer different participation rates depending upon their investment strategies and crediting methods. The participation rate can be specified for the term of the contract or for a contract year. If the rate is specified for a contract year, then the insurer will declare the participation rate each year of the annuity contract term.

Some insurers place a *cap*, or upper limit, on the amount of the index's gain in value that will be credited to the equity-indexed annuity contract. Figure 3-2 provides an example, which shows how the cap and participation rate work together with the high water mark method.

FIGURE 3.2

Crediting Excess Interest.

An equity-indexed annuity contract specifies that the participation rate for the term of the contract is 90 percent with a cap of 12 percent. Using the high water mark method, if the index value changes from 400 at the beginning of the contract term to 480 at the end of the contract year, that is a gain of 20 percent. For that contract year, the excess interest calculation would be 90 percent (the participation rate) of 20 percent (the gain in the value of the index), which is 18 percent (0.90 x 0.20 = 0.18). However, because the cap is 12 percent, the excess interest credited to this equity-indexed annuity would be 12 percent. If the value of the index had declined to 300 from a starting value of 400, no excess interest would have been credited for that contract year.

One final factor that affects excess interest is a *vesting schedule*, which is a timetable that specifies how much the contract owner can withdraw—before the end of the contract term—of the gain in the index's value that has been credited to the contract. Generally, the percentage available increases over the term of the contract. By the end of the term, the contract owner can withdraw 100 percent of the gains.

Other Contract Provisions

Many of the contract provisions that we discussed in Chapter 2 and that are found in fixed and variable annuities are also found in equity-indexed annuity contracts. Typical contract provisions for equity-indexed annuities include ones for the death benefit, withdrawals, and surrenders. Because these provisions operate similarly in fixed, variable, and equity-indexed annuities, we will not discuss them again here. We encourage you to review Chapter 2 to refresh your memory about these provisions.

Pricing Equity-Indexed Annuities

Although the calculations insurers use to price their equity-indexed annuities are beyond the scope of this text, we can make a few general points about how insurers are able to provide guaranteed interest rates and credit excess interest rates to their equity-indexed annuity contracts.

As they do for all of the premiums for their fixed annuities, insurers invest the largest portion of the equity-indexed annuity premiums in low-risk investments. The gains earned on these investments are used to pay the guaranteed interest rates on equity-indexed annuities. As we mentioned earlier, if the insurer's investments do not perform as expected and return less than the guaranteed interest rate that is specified in an equity-indexed contract, the insurer still must pay the guaranteed interest rate on that contract.

After purchasing the low-risk investments, the insurer invests the remaining premiums in such a way that a gain in the specified index will result in a return to the insurer that it can pass on to the equity-indexed annuity contract owner.

The Growth of the Equity-Indexed Annuity Market

Equity-indexed annuities are relatively new and have a small percentage of the market share. Because they are complex products to explain, equity-indexed annuities may not have been marketed as aggressively as fixed or variable annuities. If the volatility of the stock market increases, however, consumers may begin to favor equity-indexed annuities over variable annuities.

You will recall that equity-indexed annuities share in the growth of the market, while offering downside protection. In addition, contract owners can choose many different duration options and crediting methods that give investors good returns in different market conditions.

KEY TERMS AND CONCEPTS

equity-indexed annuity
principal
index
term
annual reset method
high water mark method
point-to-point method
participation rate
cap
vesting schedule

CHAPTER 4

Variable and Market Value Adjusted Annuities

After studying this chapter, you should be able to

◆ Identify the key elements of variable and market value adjusted annuities

◆ Describe the risk and return features that distinguish a variable annuity from a fixed or equity-indexed annuity

◆ Discuss the functions of a separate account and a subaccount

◆ List the various investment options available under a variable annuity

◆ Describe the purpose of asset allocation

◆ Discuss features unique to variable annuities including contract provisions, death benefits, and payout options

In the last chapter, we discussed the various features and provisions of fixed and equity-indexed annuities. In this chapter, we will turn our attention to variable annuities and market value adjusted annuities.

Variable annuities share many features with fixed and equity-indexed annuities, such as the typical contract provisions presented in Chapter 2. However, in this chapter we will focus on the features that distinguish variable annuities from fixed and equity-indexed annuities. We will discuss the various investment options and special services typically associated with variable annuities. We will also describe standard variable annuity death benefit options and payout schedules. Finally, we will take a brief look at another type of annuity—the market value adjusted annuity.

VARIABLE ANNUITIES

As we mentioned in Chapter 1, a variable annuity is a type of annuity under which (1) the investment risk is assumed by the contract owner; (2) the contract owner determines, within certain limits, how to invest his premiums; and (3) the value of the annuity depends on the performance of investments in variable subaccounts.

Let's continue our discussion of variable annuities now by looking at *risk*—which is the possibility of loss—and *return*—which is the profit or compensation an investor earns for taking a risk—and how these two elements distinguish variable annuities from fixed and equity-indexed annuities.

Investment Risk and Return

As we discussed in Chapter 3, an insurer deposits fixed and equity-indexed annuity premiums in its general account. Based on the expected performance of investments in the general account, the insurer establishes a guaranteed rate of return that it promises to pay on its fixed and equity-indexed annuity contracts. If the investments the insurer has chosen do not perform as expected, the insurer still must pay the guaranteed rate on these contracts—even if the actual rate of return is less than the guaranteed rate. In this way, the insurer assumes the risk associated with investments for fixed and equity-indexed annuity contracts.

In contrast, the investment risk for variable annuities shifts from the insurer to the contract owner. The contract owner—not the insurer—directs where and in what amounts her premiums will be invested (within the range of investment choices offered in the annuity contract). The insurer does not determine the rate of return the variable annuity contract owner will earn on her money. Instead, the performance of the investments the contract owner has chosen determines the rate of return she will earn on the money she has invested. Further, the insurer generally offers no minimum return guarantees on the contract owner's investments. In this way, the contract owner assumes the risk associated with her variable annuity investments.

Because the contract owner assumes the risk associated with her investments in the variable annuity contract, she keeps all returns the investments generate, excluding any applicable expense charges. When market conditions are favorable, a fixed annuity contract owner experiences no change in total returns because her money is "locked-in" at a fixed rate. However, under similar market conditions, a variable annuity contract owner may earn higher returns because her investment earnings are not fixed and can increase as market values rise. As a result, a variable annuity can provide a measure of protection against the effects of inflation, because it can generate a stream of income that keeps up with inflation in times when the income from a fixed annuity may not do so.

On the other hand, current and guaranteed rates protect fixed annuity investments from market downturns, while the variable annuity contract owner must absorb any losses resulting from declining market values. During periods of market decline, both the return on the investments and the overall value of the variable annuity may decline as well, resulting even in a loss of the initial investment. Insight 4-1 compares and contrasts the effects of investment performance on the value of a fixed annuity contract and a variable annuity contract.

The impact of market gains and losses on variable annuity investments and the shift of investment risk from the insurer to the contract owner are distinctive features of variable annuities. Together, these features represent the most significant differences between variable and fixed annuities.

In addition, because the investment risk shifts from the insurer to the contract owner, variable annuities, unlike fixed annuities, are considered securities in the United States. As securities, variable annuities must be registered with the *Securities and Exchange Commission (SEC)*, which is an agency of the U.S. government charged with regulating transactions in financial securities. Insurers who issue and administer variable annuity contracts must abide by the laws and rules that govern securities and securities trading. We will discuss the regulations that apply to both variable and fixed annuity products in more detail in Chapter 8.

The Separate Account

As we mentioned earlier, an insurer deposits fixed and equity-indexed annuity premiums in its general account. Premiums for variable annuity

| INSIGHT 4.1 | **Effects of Investment Performance on Fixed Annuity and Variable Annuity Returns.** |

On January 1, Pamela Chase and her sister, Paula, each purchased a $10,000 deferred annuity from the Auburn Life Insurance Company. Pamela purchased a fixed annuity with a one-year interest rate set at 6 percent; Paula purchased a variable annuity with no interest rate guarantees.

During the period from January 1 to December 31 of that year, market values rose steadily and Auburn Life was able to earn a total return of 10 percent on the investments in its general account. When Auburn Life credited interest to its one-year fixed annuity contracts on December 31, the value of Pamela's fixed annuity increased by 6 percent, from $10,000 to $10,600. She realized no additional gain as a result of the performance of the investments in Auburn Life's general account.

As for Paula, the value of her variable annuity also increased at the end of the year. Earnings on the subaccounts Paula had chosen for her variable annuity rose with the market. Like the investments in Auburn Life's general account, Paula's variable annuity subaccount investments also earned a total return of 10 percent for the year. Thus, Paula's variable annuity increased in value from $10,000 to $11,000—$400 more than the gain realized on Pamela's fixed annuity. By foregoing fixed interest rate guarantees, Paula was able to realize a larger gain in value as a result of favorable market conditions during the year.

Now, consider another scenario. Assuming all other factors remained the same, what would happen if market values declined during the period from January 1 to December 31 and Auburn Life was able to earn a return of only 5 percent on the investments in its general account? Pamela would still earn a fixed rate of 6 percent and the value of her annuity would increase to $10,600. However, if Paula's investment earnings once again moved with the market, she would earn a return of only 5 percent on her annuity. With no interest rate guarantee, the value of Paula's variable annuity would increase to only $10,500—$100 less than the gain realized on Pamela's fixed annuity. While a return of 5 percent still represents a gain for Paula, if market values continue to decline in subsequent years, the overall value of Paula's annuity could decline as well, eventually dropping below the $10,000 value of her initial investment.

contracts, however, are not put in the insurer's general account. Instead, variable annuity premium payments are deposited in a separate account. As we noted in Chapter 1, a separate account is an investment account that is independent from the insurer's general account. The separate account provides the insurer with a means to keep the premiums that fund traditional insurance products separate from the premiums that fund variable insurance products. Further, unlike assets held in the insurer's general account, assets in the separate account are not subject to the claims of the insurer's creditors.

Subaccounts

As we mentioned in Chapter 1, a subaccount, also known as a *variable investment account* or a *variable subaccount*, is the means by which variable annuity contract owners invest their premiums within the separate account. The investment needs of contract owners vary depending on their goals, financial situations, risk tolerance, and other personal factors. As a result, insurers generally offer a wide variety of subaccount investment options in their variable annuity contracts. These subaccount options represent investments in an array of financial instruments and encompass varying levels of risk and return. A typical variable annuity might offer a selection of 10 or more different variable subaccounts. In addition, contract owners can usually place a portion of premiums in a guaranteed subaccount. A *fixed account*, sometimes called a *variable guaranteed account*, guarantees payment of a fixed rate of interest for a specified period of time. Unlike other variable subaccount investments, money invested in the fixed account is held in the insurer's general account.

Subaccounts function much like mutual funds and are subject to many of the same regulations as mutual funds. A *mutual fund* is an account established by a financial services company that combines the money of many people and invests it in a variety of financial instruments. However, do not confuse an insurer's variable annuity subaccounts with mutual funds that may have the same or similar names. Mutual funds and variable annuity subaccounts are always separate investment entities and are treated very differently for tax purposes. Like their mutual fund counterparts though, variable annuity subaccounts have similar investment objectives and invest in the same types of financial instruments.

At the time she purchases a variable annuity, the contract owner must select at least one subaccount in which to invest annuity premiums. If the contract owner chooses more than one subaccount, she must specify what percentage of premiums she wishes to invest in each subaccount. The insurer will distribute the initial premium payment and any additional premiums to the specified subaccounts in the percentages indicated. For example, suppose that Joan Hall chooses to invest her premium payments in four subaccounts as indicated below:

- ◆ 40 percent to Subaccount A
- ◆ 25 percent to Subaccount B
- ◆ 20 percent to Subaccount C
- ◆ 15 percent to Subaccount D

If Ms. Hall makes an initial premium payment of $2,000, the insurer would invest $800 in Subaccount A, $500 in Subaccount B, $400 in Subaccount C, and $300 in Subaccount D.

After the annuity has been issued, the contract owner may (1) transfer money between subaccounts, (2) change the percentage of premiums allocated to specific subaccounts, or (3) change the subaccounts in which future premiums are invested.

Accumulation Units

The contract owner invests premiums in a variable annuity subaccount by purchasing shares of a subaccount's holdings. As you will recall from our discussion in Chapter 2, these ownership shares are called **accumulation units**. The number of accumulation units that a given premium will purchase depends on the unit value when the premium is paid. The value, or price, of an accumulation unit on a given day is equal to the market value of a subaccount's invested assets at the end of the previous day divided by the number of outstanding accumulation units in the subaccount. Figure 4-1 demonstrates how to calculate accumulation unit values.

FIGURE 4.1

Calculating Accumulation Unit Value.

At the close of business on June 1, Variable Subaccount A has a market value of $500,000 and 25,000 units outstanding. Therefore, on June 2 the value of an accumulation unit in Variable Subaccount A is $20.00.

$$\left(\begin{array}{c}\text{Market value of}\\\text{invested assets}\end{array}\right) \div \left(\begin{array}{c}\text{Accumulation units}\\\text{outstanding}\end{array}\right) = \left(\begin{array}{c}\text{Accumulation unit}\\\text{value/price}\end{array}\right)$$

| $500,000 | ÷ | 25,000 | = | $20.00 |

On June 2, a $100 premium will purchase five accumulation units in Variable Subaccount A.

$$\left(\begin{array}{c}\text{Premium}\\\text{payment}\end{array}\right) \div \left(\begin{array}{c}\text{Accumulation unit}\\\text{value/price}\end{array}\right) = \left(\begin{array}{c}\text{Accumulation}\\\text{units purchased}\end{array}\right)$$

| $100.00 | ÷ | $20.00 | = | 5 |

Each time a contract owner pays premiums, those premiums purchase accumulation units at current prices, and the total number of accumulation units in the account gradually increases. The value of a contract owner's investment in a variable annuity subaccount depends on both the current value of an accumulation unit and the number of accumulation units held.

For example, as Figure 4-2 illustrates, the value of 100 accumulation units in a variable annuity subaccount is equal to $500 when the current value of an accumulation unit is $5.00. If the value of an accumulation unit drops to $3.00, the value of the annuity investment will drop to $300. However, if the value of an accumulation unit rises to $8.00, then the value of the annuity investment will increase to $800.

In Figure 4-2, the number of accumulation units remains constant, but the value of the subaccount fluctuates. This fluctuation results from changes

---

FIGURE 4.2

Calculating Subaccount Values.

$$\left(\begin{array}{c}\text{Number of}\\\text{accumulation units}\end{array}\right) \times \left(\begin{array}{c}\text{Accumulation}\\\text{unit value}\end{array}\right) = \left(\begin{array}{c}\text{Subaccount}\\\text{value}\end{array}\right)$$

100	×	$3.00	=	$300
100	×	$5.00	=	$500
100	×	$8.00	=	$800

in the value of an accumulation unit, in turn resulting from changes in the market value of the underlying investments. Through this valuation mechanism, market performance affects the value of the contract owner's investment in a variable annuity. Keep in mind, increasing or decreasing the number of accumulation units held in a subaccount can also change the value of the contract owner's investment. See Insight 4-2 for a detailed discussion of accumulation unit values and variable annuity subaccount values.

INSIGHT 4.2

Accumulation Units and Variable Annuity Subaccount Values.

On April 30, Scott James purchased a variable deferred annuity and selected Subaccount A as the investment vehicle for his annuity. Over a three-month period, the value of an accumulation unit in Subaccount A was as follows:

April 30..........$2.00   May 30..........$3.00   June 30..........$2.50

Scott paid a premium of $600 in each of these three months.

APRIL	MAY	JUNE
On April 30, the $600 premium purchased 300 accumulation units ($600 ÷ $2.00 = 300)	**On May 30, the $600 premium purchased 200 accumulation units ($600 ÷ $3.00 = 200)**	**On June 30, the $600 premium purchased 240 accumulation units ($600 ÷ $2.50 = 240)**
Total Premium Invested $600.00	Total Premium Invested ... $1,200.00 ($600 + $600 = $1,200)	Total Premium Invested ... $1,800.00 ($600 + $600 + $600 = $1,800)
Total Units Purchased 300	Total Units Purchased .... 500 (300 + 200 = 500)	Total Units Purchased .... 740 (300 + 200 + 240 = 740)
Current Value of an Accumulation Unit $2.00	Current Value of an Accumulation Unit $3.00	Current Value of an Accumulation Unit $2.50
Current Value of Scott's Annuity .... $600.00 (300 × $2.00 = $600)	Current Value of Scott's Annuity .... $1,500.00 (500 × $3.00 = $1,500)	Current Value of Scott's Annuity $1,850.00

Over the three-month period, the $1,800 that Scott paid in premiums was sufficient to purchase a total of 740 accumulation units. Due to changing market conditions during this time period, the investment performance of Subaccount A fluctuated, causing accumulation unit values to vary from month to month. These fluctuations affected not only how much Scott paid for each accumulation unit in Subaccount A, but also the number of accumulation units each premium payment purchased. In turn, these factors determined the total value of Scott's investment in Subaccount A at the end of each month.

Asset Classes

The subaccount investments in a typical variable annuity contract provide the contract owner with a number of options. Some subaccount investments attempt to preserve principal while providing a steady stream of income. Recall from Chapter 3 that principal is the total amount the contract owner has invested in the annuity, exclusive of any investment returns. Other subaccount investments focus more on long-term growth and capital appreciation. **Capital appreciation** is an increase in the market value of invested assets. Regardless of the number of subaccount options offered and the variety of investment objectives represented, all of the underlying investments of a variable annuity's subaccounts will fall into one of three broad asset classes. An *asset class* is a group of similar investment instruments linked by related risk and return features. The three asset classes we will consider in relation to variable annuity subaccounts are (1) money markets, (2) bonds, and (3) stocks.

Money Market Subaccount. A *money market subaccount* in an insurance company's separate account is an asset class in which shares are typically invested in short-term money instruments or cash equivalents, such as United States Treasury bills. Money market instruments generally carry the least risk for the investor, but also tend to generate lower returns than either bond or stock investments.

Bond Subaccount. A *bond subaccount* in an insurance company's separate account is an asset class in which shares are typically invested in a variety of both short-term and long-term government and corporate bonds. A *bond* is a type of debt that reflects money the issuer has borrowed and must repay to the bond-holder. Bonds and money market instruments both generate regular income in the form of *interest*—fees that bond issuers, banks, and other financial institutions pay for the use of borrowed money. Bonds generally offer greater returns than do money market instruments, but bond values tend to fluctuate more than the value of money market instruments in response to market conditions. Therefore, bonds also involve a greater amount of risk for the investor.

Stock Subaccount. A *stock subaccount* in an insurance company's separate account is an asset class in which shares are typically invested in an array of domestic and foreign stocks. A *stock* is an ownership share in a company. Stocks generate income in the form of dividends. A *dividend* is a stockowner's share of a company's profits; dividends may rise or fall based on a company's perfor-mance. Stocks may also appreciate—or depreciate—in value, depending on market conditions. Because stock prices vary greatly and fluctuate as cor-porate and market conditions change, stocks tend to carry the greatest risk for investors. Stocks also offer a higher potential return than either bonds or money market instruments.

Generally, all variable annuity subaccounts try to minimize risk by diversifying investment holdings. *Diversification* is the process of investing in a number of financial instruments within an asset class to minimize the risk associated with any one investment or type of investment. Through diversification, positive returns earned from some investments held in the subaccount may offset the negative impact of one or more poorly performing investments.

Investment Options

The types and number of subaccounts offered under a variable annuity contract vary from insurer to insurer. Most insurers, however, offer sub-accounts representing each of the asset classes presented here—money markets, bonds, and stocks—and many offer more than one subaccount within each asset class.

The names and subaccount classifications used within variable annuity contracts also differ from insurer to insurer; however, the general categories and types of subaccounts are fairly similar. Figure 4-3 presents a list of money market, bond, and stock subaccounts commonly found in variable annuity contracts sold by U.S. insurers.

FIGURE 4.3

Variable Annuity Subaccounts.

Asset Class	Subaccount Name	Typical Investments
Money Market	Money Market	U.S. Treasury bills
Bond	Government	Obligations of the U.S. government and its agencies
	Corporate	Bonds issued by U.S. corporations
	International	Bonds issued by foreign governments and corporations
Stock	Large Cap	Stocks of large U.S. corporations
	Mid Cap	Stocks of medium-sized U.S. corporations
	Small Cap	Stocks of small U.S. corporations
	Value	Stocks of U.S. corporations currently priced below market value
	Growth	Stocks of U.S. corporations demonstrating strong potential for capital appreciation
	Income	Stocks of U.S. corporations with a stable dividend payment history
	Growth & Income	A mixture of stocks of U.S. corporations demonstrating strong potential for capital appreciation and stocks of U.S. corporations with a stable dividend payment history
	International	Stocks of foreign corporations
	Global	Stocks of both foreign and U.S. corporations
Money Market, Bond, Stock	Sector	Stocks or bonds from a particular industry or market segment (such as telecommunications, utilities, health care)
	Index	Stocks or bonds that make up one of the financial market indices
	Fixed or Guaranteed	General account
	Balanced or Asset Allocation	A mix of money market instruments, bonds, and stocks

Asset Allocation

Investing exclusively in either money market, bond, or stock instruments can help an investor meet many financial goals. However, combining investments in each of these asset classes can help minimize exposure to risk. The process of investing in money markets, bonds, and stocks in predetermined proportions is known as *asset allocation*.

Variable annuity contracts offer investors a built-in opportunity to realize the benefits of asset allocation. By depositing premiums into several sub-accounts, and including each asset class in the total distribution, contract owners can establish asset mixes with risk and return features that match their personal financial needs and objectives. In addition, contract owners can change the asset allocation periodically to match new or changing investment goals. In this way, asset allocation allows the investor to build a *portfolio*, which is a diversified collection of financial instruments that aligns specific investment strategies with the financial goals of an investor.

Asset Allocation Models

When deciding on an asset mix, investors must consider

- ◆ Their tolerance for risk
- ◆ The level of investment return they desire
- ◆ Their investment time frame

In general, money market investments are the least risky for the investor, but offer the lowest returns. Bonds are riskier, but offer better returns, particularly if interest rates decline. Stocks are generally the riskiest investments, but offer the potential for the highest returns. This interplay between risk and return—higher risks usually generate higher returns and lower risks usually generate lower returns—is known as the *risk-return trade-off*. In addition, the longer an investor can leave invested assets untouched, the greater risk he can afford to take.

To help variable annuity contract owners choose an asset mix that matches their investment objectives, many insurers offer asset allocation models. In this context, an *asset allocation model* is a tool that uses an investor's personal and financial data to generate options for strategically distributing assets among different types and classes of investments. A typical asset allocation model might require input regarding a contract owner's age group, tax bracket, current income, investment objectives, time constraints, risk tolerance, and the amount of other investments or financial obligations. The asset allocation model suggests an appropriate mix of assets that takes into consideration all these factors. A contract owner can then apply the resulting asset allocation by proportionally allocating premiums to corresponding subaccounts within the variable annuity contract. The contract owner chooses the actual allocations, mix of assets, and sub-accounts, and may or may not follow the asset allocation model suggestions. Figure 4-4 presents three representative asset allocation models and their corresponding risk and return characteristics.

Special Services

Often, an insurance company issuing variable annuity contracts will offer special services to contract owners. Typically these *special services* are contract

FIGURE 4.4

Asset Allocation Models.

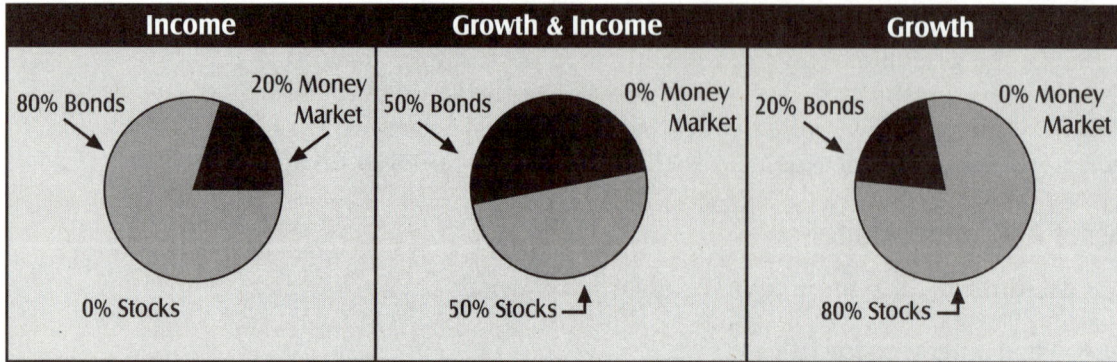

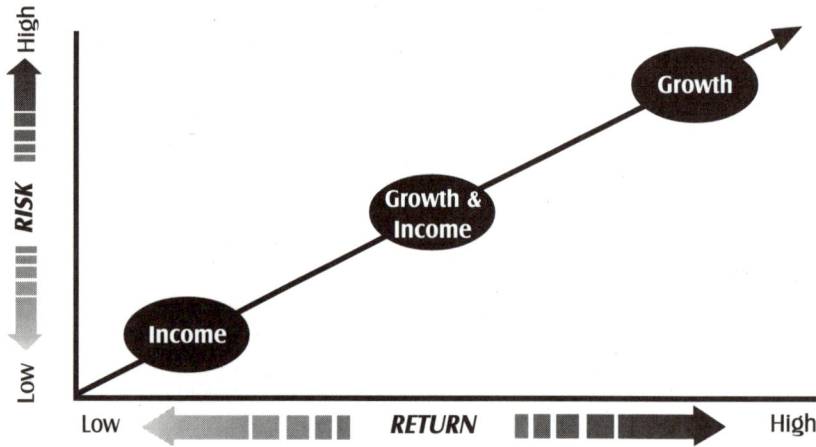

Income	Growth & Income	Growth

80% Bonds
20% Money Market
0% Stocks

50% Bonds
0% Money Market
50% Stocks

20% Bonds
0% Money Market
80% Stocks

High
RISK
Low

Growth

Growth & Income

Income

Low — RETURN — High

provisions designed to help contract owners more efficiently manage their variable subaccount investments. Three special service provisions included in most variable annuity contracts are (1) automatic dollar cost averaging, (2) transfers between subaccounts, and (3) automatic rebalancing.

Automatic Dollar Cost Averaging

Investing a fixed dollar amount in one or more financial instruments on a regular, periodic basis is known as *dollar cost averaging*. Under the *automatic dollar cost averaging* provision, variable annuity contract owners generally deposit their premiums directly into a variable annuity's fixed account or money market subaccount, although any subaccount may be used. The deposits then periodically purchase accumulation units in one or more of the annuity's other subaccounts.

Over time, automatic dollar cost averaging enables contract owners to systematically purchase more accumulation units when unit prices are low and fewer units when unit prices are high. This investment strategy reduces the average price of accumulation units purchased, thereby reducing costs to the contract owner and increasing the amount of the contract owner's investment available to earn returns.

Transfers Between Subaccounts

Transfers are a special service that allow contract owners to move assets between variable annuity subaccounts during the accumulation phase as well as during the payout period. The ability to shift assets from one subaccount to another enables the contract owner to respond to changing market conditions and to adjust asset allocations to meet changing financial needs and investment objectives. Most variable annuity contracts include some restrictions regarding the maximum number and minimum dollar amount of subaccount transfers a contract owner may authorize during the accumulation phase. Some contracts may require the contract owner to pay a fee if requested transfers exceed designated limits. In addition, when the payout period has begun, most variable annuity contracts do not allow contract owners to make transfers in and out of the fixed account. The contracts may also limit transfers among the other subaccounts to certain designated dates.

Automatic Rebalancing

In Chapter 2, we mentioned the automatic rebalancing service, which allows for an automatic transfer of assets between subaccounts in order to maintain the asset allocation balance the contract owner has specified. As we have noted, variable annuity contract owners must specify what proportions of each premium payment to allocate to each subaccount within the annuity. Fluctuations in subaccount values and varying rates of return on investments can have a significant impact on the actual proportion of total assets invested in each particular subaccount. In other words, the proportional distribution of assets in the subaccounts may not always equal the proportional distribution of assets the contract owner specified at the time the annuity was purchased.

For example, assume that Jim West purchased a variable deferred annuity from the Juniper Life Insurance Company with a single premium payment of $50,000. At the time he purchased the annuity, Jim elected to invest 50 percent of the premium in Stock Subaccount A and 50 percent of the premium in Bond Subaccount B. Later that year, stock values increased and bond earnings dropped. The investments in Stock Subaccount A began earning a higher rate of return, while the value of the investments in Bond Subaccount B began to decline. As a result, the proportion of Jim's invested assets in Stock Subaccount A gradually increased to 60 percent of his total investment and the proportion of his invested assets in Bond Subaccount B decreased to 40 percent of his total investment. Thus, the proportional distribution of Jim's invested assets no longer reflected his original asset allocation. If Jim wished to maintain the original asset allocation on his own, he would have to continually monitor the performance and value of his subaccount investments and transfer assets back and forth as necessary. An automatic rebalancing provision would ensure that funds from Stock Subaccount A would be periodically transferred to Bond Subaccount B in order to maintain Jim's original 50/50 asset allocation split.

Death Benefit

As we have seen, excluding any money held in fixed accounts, variable annuities do not provide guarantees with regard to interest rates or safety of principal. However, as we mentioned in Chapter 2, variable annuity contracts often do include a minimum death benefit guarantee. The death benefit guarantee protects the contract owner against the loss of principal invested in a variable annuity and in some cases even protects the contract owner against the loss of investment earnings.

For example, assume that Robert Smith purchased a single premium deferred annuity with a $50,000 payment on January 2. He named his wife Loretta as the beneficiary. On March 3, during the annuity's accumulation period, Robert died without having made any withdrawals from the annuity. On the date of his death, the value of the subaccounts in his variable annuity had fallen to $40,000 because of poor investment performance. The value of the death benefit paid to his wife, however, would be equal to the amount of premiums paid—in this case, $50,000. If the value of Robert's annuity at the time of his death had increased to $60,000, his wife would receive the total account value, or $60,000.

While the preceding example describes the most common way to calculate variable annuity death benefits, some insurers offer variations on these guarantees. For instance, the contract owner may choose to have the account value determined using a date other than the date of death, such as the last policy anniversary date. Further, some contracts offer a guaranteed growth option. Under this option, the insurer agrees to credit a minimum interest rate (usually 3 to 5 percent) on premiums if the total account value at the time of death is equal to or less than the sum of premiums paid.

Payout Period

As a fixed annuity does, a variable annuity allows the contract owner to determine how money will be paid out at the end of the accumulation period. As we discussed in Chapter 2, the contract owner can choose from a number of payout options: fixed period, fixed amount, life, life income with period certain, life income with refund, and joint and survivor. Unlike the fixed annuity contract owner, however, the variable annuity contract owner faces additional choices concerning how money will be paid out under any one of these options.

At the end of the accumulation period, a variable annuity contract owner has three choices with regard to receiving annuity payments: (1) he can elect to receive payments that will be fixed throughout the payout period,

(2) he can choose to receive all of the payments under a variable payout option, or (3) he can choose to receive part of the payments under a fixed payout option and part under a variable payout option.

Fixed Payout Option

If the variable annuity contract owner chooses the fixed payout option, the insurer makes a series of payments to the payee that are of a fixed amount throughout the payout period. Under this option, the insurer transfers the accumulated value of the annuity from the separate account to its general account. The value of the annuity depends on the number and value of accumulation units the contract owner holds in the various variable annuity subaccounts. The accumulation units are, in effect, "cashed in" and the money is distributed to the payee in a series of equal annuity payments. The amount of the annuity payments depends on the accumulated value of the annuity, the payout period selected, and the insurer's current and guaranteed interest rates.

Variable Payout Option

The variable annuity contract owner may also choose to receive annuity payments under a variable payout option. When the contract owner selects the variable payout option, the insurer makes a series of payments to the payee that vary throughout the payout period. Under this option, the accumulated value of the annuity remains in the separate account. The annuity's accumulation units are not "cashed in"—they are instead converted to annuity units. **Annuity units** are shares in an insurer's separate account that determine the size of future annuity payments after the income date has been reached. The insurer establishes the number of annuity units it will credit to a contract owner before making the first annuity payment. The accumulated value of the annuity and the current value of an annuity unit determine the number of annuity units the insurer will credit to the contract owner. Annuity unit values vary from one subaccount to another. Therefore, the number of annuity units credited to a contract owner will also depend on the subaccount or subaccounts in which she places her accumulated assets.

During the payout period, the contract owner may allocate annuity units among variable subaccounts in much the same way she allocated premiums during the accumulation phase. Exchanging annuity units between subaccounts may result in either an increase or a decrease in the number of annuity units, depending on the unit value of each subaccount.

Annuity units, like accumulation units, fluctuate in value because of changes in the value of subaccount investments. Because the value of annuity units varies, annuity payments will vary throughout the payout period.

For example, assume Ann Gold has 100 annuity units in Subaccount Z on the income date of her variable deferred annuity contract. If the value of an annuity unit in Subaccount Z is $5.00 on the date the insurer makes its first monthly annuity payment to Ann, the annuity payment will be $500 ($5.00 × 100). However, if the value of an annuity unit in Subaccount Z falls to $4.75 on the date the insurer makes its next monthly annuity payment to Ann, the annuity payment will be only $475 ($4.75 × 100). On the other hand, if the value of an annuity unit in Subaccount Z increases to $5.25 on this date, then the monthly annuity payment the insurer makes to Ann will be $525 ($5.25 × 100).

Keep in mind that this example of annuity unit calculations is overly simplified. In reality, a number of other factors, which are beyond the scope of this text, also affect the calculation of annuity payments.

Fixed and Variable Payout Option

As we mentioned in Chapter 2, the variable annuity contract owner also may choose to combine a fixed payout with a variable payout. Under this option, the insurer transfers a portion of the accumulated value of the annuity to its general account. This portion of the annuity's accumulated value will provide regular and fixed annuity payments. The insurer converts the remainder of the annuity's accumulated value to annuity units, and the contract owner invests this portion in one or more variable subaccounts within the separate account. This portion of the annuity's accumulated value will provide an annuity payment that will vary depending on the performance of investments in the chosen subaccounts. The contract owner can choose any proportions he desires for the split. Once the contract owner establishes the proportions, however, he cannot transfer assets between the fixed and variable portions of the annuity.

No matter which payout option the contract owner selects—fixed, variable, or fixed and variable—he must also choose the terms of the payout (for example, life with period certain); select the frequency of the payment (for example, monthly); and, with a variable payout option, elect from which subaccounts the annuity payments will be made.

Assumed Investment Return

Most variable annuity contracts also specify an ***assumed investment return (AIR)***, which is the total return that the subaccount investments must earn in order for annuity payments to remain the same throughout the payout period. The AIR is used to calculate the initial annuity payment and to project future annuity payments under the annuity. If the return on the underlying subaccount investments is less than the AIR, the annuity payments will decrease. If the return is greater, annuity payments will increase. Actual AIR calculations used to arrive at the monthly annuity payment are highly complex and are beyond the scope of this text. Most states have limitations on AIRs, but the most commonly used AIRs are 3 percent and 5 percent. Under some variable annuity contracts, the contract owner can select the AIR from within a certain range.

Figure 4-5 presents a brief summary of the distinctions between fixed annuities and variable annuities that we have presented and discussed in this chapter.

FIGURE 4.5

Fixed Annuities and Variable Annuities.

FEATURES	FIXED	VARIABLE
Return to contract owner	Fixed over specified period	Fluctuates based on actual investment results
Guarantees to contract owner	Rate guaranteed for specified period; also guaranteed minimum rate	No investment guarantees on variable subaccounts
Funds invested in...	General account	Separate account
Investment risk assumed by...	Insurer	Contract owner
Payout option	Fixed	Owner chooses fixed, variable, or fixed and variable

MARKET VALUE ADJUSTED ANNUITIES

A *market value adjusted annuity* is an annuity that features fixed interest rate guarantees combined with an interest rate adjustment factor that can cause the actual rate credited to fluctuate in response to market conditions. In addition, insurers sometimes include a market value adjustment feature in other types of annuity products. For example, an insurer might link a market value adjustment to one or more of the guarantee periods offered under a fixed annuity or to one or more of the guarantee periods associated with a variable annuity's fixed account.

A market value adjustment works by allowing the contract owner to place money in an account earning a fixed rate of interest. The insurer holds the contract owner's money in this account for a designated period of time—the guarantee period. The insurer specifies a basis on which it will establish market value adjustments. The insurer may tie this figure to interest rates or the performance of a particular market index. As long as the contract owner leaves all money in the account until the end of the guarantee period, the value of invested assets will increase at the fixed rate. If, however, the contract owner decides to remove some or all of the money from the account before the end of the guarantee period, a market value adjustment will apply and the account value will either increase or decrease depending on the prevailing market rates. Most insurers allow for partial withdrawals—up to a specified percent of total account value—with no adjustment. In addition, if the withdrawal is made within a specified period of time preceding the end of the guarantee period—usually 30 days—no market value adjustment will apply. The insurer determines the market value adjustment by comparing the account's fixed rate to the prevailing market rate or to the performance of a specified market index. The actual calculation used to determine the market value adjustment is complex and beyond the scope of this text.

The market value adjustment reflects changes in market interest rates that affect the value of the financial instruments backing the insurer's fixed interest rate guarantees. The most common types of financial instruments used to back fixed interest rate guarantees on annuity products are bonds and money market instruments. When interest rates rise, existing bonds and money market instruments decrease in value because investors can earn higher rates by purchasing bonds and money market instruments at prevailing market rates. Similarly, when interest rates fall, existing bonds and money market instruments increase in value because investors can earn a higher return on these investments than they can on bonds and money market instruments issued at the prevailing market rates.

Market interest rates determine the prices at which an insurer can sell bonds and money market instruments to accommodate withdrawals from market value adjusted annuity accounts. When the prevailing market interest rate is higher than the fixed interest rate specified in the annuity contract, an insurer may have to sell certain financial instruments at a loss in order to accommodate account withdrawals. Under these circumstances, a negative market value adjustment occurs when a contract owner withdraws money from his annuity. In other words, the contract owner will lose a portion of investment earnings or—depending on provisions contained in the contract—a portion of the initial investment.

On the other hand, when the prevailing market interest rate is lower than the fixed interest rate specified in the annuity contract, an insurer may be able to generate significant returns from the sale of certain financial instruments. Under these circumstances, a positive market value adjustment will occur when a contract owner withdraws moneys from his account. In other words, the contract owner will realize an additional gain above the fixed interest rate specified in the annuity contract.

Aside from the distinctions presented herein, market value adjusted annuities are similar in many ways to the other types of annuities we have looked at. Market value adjusted annuities contain the same types of contract provisions regarding death benefits and payout options we have already discussed.

KEY TERMS AND CONCEPTS

risk
return
Securities and Exchange Commission (SEC)
fixed account
mutual fund

capital appreciation
asset class
money market subaccount
bond subaccount
bond
interest
stock subaccount
stock
dividend
diversification
asset allocation
portfolio
risk-return trade-off
asset allocation model
special services
dollar cost averaging
automatic dollar cost averaging
transfers
annuity units
assumed investment return (AIR)
market value adjusted annuity

CHAPTER 5

Annuities and Investments

After studying this chapter, you should be able to

◆ Discuss the effect of a person's risk tolerance on investing

◆ Describe the risks associated with annuity contracts

◆ Discuss the importance of the time value of money to investing

◆ Discuss investment strategies including dollar cost averaging, diversification, and asset allocation

◆ Compare annuities to other financial services products

Annuity products can be part of an investor's portfolio. Although we will not specifically address the process of financial planning, we will cover several important issues that an investor should consider when developing an investment strategy. First, we will discuss the trade-off between risk and return in any investment. Then, we will explain how the investor's time horizon helps dictate the types of products that may be appropriate to include in an investment portfolio. We also will cover other issues relating to the development of an investment strategy, including investment principles such as the time value of money, diversification, and asset allocation. Finally, we will describe how annuities compare to other types of financial service products.

DEALING WITH RISK

As we have already mentioned, fixed annuities attract investors who are interested in interest rate guarantees. In contrast, variable annuities offer the opportunity for higher returns than those offered by fixed or even equity-indexed annuities to contract owners who are willing to assume the associated risk. To varying degrees, risk is inherent in every savings, investment, or insurance product. For example, when a person purchases shares of stock, she hopes that the price of the stock will go up, that her initial investment will grow, and that she will earn a profit. However, she is taking a risk that the price of the stock will fall and that she may lose some or all of the money she invested. Or, the price of the stock may remain unchanged and she will neither lose nor make money.

On the other hand, if that same investor purchases a *certificate of deposit (CD)*—a contractual agreement issued by a bank that returns the investor's principal with interest on a specified date— her money is guaranteed (up to $100,000) by a federal government agency that ensures that even if the bank fails, the investor's money will be safe. Investing in CDs is not entirely without risk. If the entire economy of the United States failed and the government went bankrupt, then the bank might have difficulty paying the investor her money. However, the chance of such an event occurring is so remote that investors ignore the small amount of risk in such an investment. On the other hand, because of the low risk associated with a CD, it generally does not pay as high a rate of return as an investment in stocks has the potential to pay.

Investing and Risk Tolerance

Learning to make wise choices when investing money requires understanding the relationship between risk and return. A person's willingness or unwillingness to accept a certain degree of risk can affect the amount of income—or return—that he can earn on a certain savings or investment product. You will recall from our discussion in Chapter 4 that risk and return are directly related—the higher the potential degree of risk in a product, the higher the potential for return. Conversely, the lower the potential degree of risk, the lower the potential for reward or return. Figure 5-1 contains a quiz that

---

FIGURE 5.1

Investment Risk Strategy Quiz.

Do you want to put money away and take as little risk as possible or do you want to put your money to work and assume a bit more risk? Maybe you want to be somewhere in the middle. Before you choose your investment selections you should determine a strategy.

Here's a quick quiz to help you identify how much risk you may be comfortable taking with your investments. Remember, this is only a general guideline to help you determine a possible investment strategy and be sure that you are comfortable with whatever investment decisions you make.

Read through each question and enter your answer in the box to the right of the question. When you've finished, add up the numbers in the boxes to get your "risk tolerance" score. Then you will be ready to figure out a strategy and choose the investment options that are right for you.

A. How old are you?

20–29	30–39	40–49	50–59	60 or over
5	4	3	2	1

B. How many years until you retire?

5	10	15	20	25 or more
1	2	3	4	5

C. Many types of investments involve significant ups and downs in the total value of your account, especially in the short term. How willing are you to ride out the following _losses_ in your account?

Down 5% or less	Down 10%	Down 15%	Down 20 % or more
1	2	3	4

D. Do you consider yourself knowledgeable about investments and do you believe that there are many advantages to investing in the stock market?

Strongly Agree	Agree	Neutral	Disagree	Strongly Disagree
5	4	3	2	1

E. Do you understand the trade-off between risk and potential reward and are you willing to accept more risk to possibly achieve higher returns?

Strongly Agree	Agree	Neutral	Disagree	Strongly Disagree
5	4	3	2	1

F. Do you feel that given your current income level and assets (e.g., home equity, IRAs, savings accounts), you will achieve your retirement goals?

Strongly Agree	Agree	Neutral	Disagree	Strongly Disagree
5	4	3	2	1

Total Score

Figure 5.1 Investment Risk Strategy Quiz *continued*

What type of strategy are your comfortable with? From the quiz, see where your score falls and place a check mark next to the strategy that best matches your tolerance for risk:

( ) **26–29 points**   *Aggressive Strategy (high risk):* You want to maximize the long-term growth of your retirement savings. You understand the ups and downs of stocks and are comfortable with taking a lot of risk to maximize returns. You have plenty of time to wait out the stock market cycles.

( ) **21–25 points**   *Growth Strategy:* You are looking to grow your money by investing and may have more time on your side. You are somewhat comfortable riding out the ups and downs of the stock market in exchange for the possibility of higher long-term results.

( ) **16–20 points**   *Balanced Strategy:* You want a balance between growth and security. You will accept some risk in order to have the potential for higher returns over time.

( ) **11–15 points**   *Moderate Strategy:* You feel a strong need to protect and grow your assets with emphasis on security. You are cautious but may be willing to diversify to spread out some of your risk.

( ) **6–10 points**   *Conservative Strategy (low risk):* Security is your most important concern. You may be approaching retirement or simply prefer to preserve more of your initial investment.

Source: Excerpted from Manulife Financial's *Your Guide to Building Financial Security.* Reprinted with permission.

helps participants in one group retirement plan identify their risk tolerance levels and select the most appropriate investment risk strategy.

In Chapter 4, we discussed how variable annuities offer the potential for greater returns than fixed annuities because the contract owner assumes the investment risk. Just as when she considers investing in any other savings, insurance, or investment product, a person purchasing an annuity should make sure that the type of annuity she purchases possesses a degree of risk that she can comfortably accept.

In addition to his personal level of comfort with risk, a person needs to consider his age and investment time frame to determine the types of savings and investment products that are appropriate. The younger the person, the more time he has to accumulate funds to provide a future income stream. A younger person also can afford to take a greater risk than an older person in order to achieve a larger possible return. For example, if a person is saving for his retirement in 35 years, a more appropriate choice may be a variable annuity or an investment with a potential for a larger return rather than a bank savings account with its lower level of risk. The closer the person gets to retirement (or the time period when he would otherwise need the accumulated funds), the more he may consider shifting some funds toward more conservative choices. Of course, "conservative" is a relative term. As Insight 5-1 points out, even seniors in retirement may need to retain some more aggressive funds in their portfolios as a hedge against inflation and to provide for the growth of their account should they live a long life.

Many books that cover life cycle investment strategies are available, so we will not discuss this topic in detail. However, you should know that a person's investment strategies may change as the person's circumstances

INSIGHT 5.1

Insurers Say Seniors Should Keep Some Risk in Their Investments.

As longevity increases and retirement ages drop, insurers are adapting their investment products to include more aggressive and flexible vehicles.

Experts say older people are showing a newfound acceptance of risk. The experts cite various reasons for this, but they give most of the credit to public realization that people must hedge against inflation.

Ted Benna, president of the 401(k) Association, a Langhorne, Pa., defined contribution consulting firm, explained that people must now consider that they may live over 30 years in retirement. "In the past you retired at 65 and lived 10 years," he said.

A man aged 65 can expect to live to be 80 or 81, and a 65-year-old woman can reasonably hope to reach 85, noted Scott Dunn, assistant scientist at LIMRA International, Windsor, Conn.

Retirees should avoid being unduly conservative in their asset allocation, said Bob Howley, a pension actuary at Buck Consultants in New York. Even a low inflation rate of 3 percent annually would more than halve the value of money over 25 years, he said.

Older Americans do need to keep at least part of their assets liquid, in order to cover sudden expenses, like emergency medical care, said Ron Goldman, an independent financial planner and sales desk director at First Penn Pacific, Oakbrook Terrace, Ill. However, he said he advises his senior financial planning clients to keep at least part of their assets in aggressive holdings.

Where should they put this type of money? Mr. Benna said variable annuities (VAs) are optimal insurance products for retirees looking to invest more aggressively.

VAs have become increasingly popular with retirees, observes Mr. Dunn. According to a recent LIMRA study of Americans who bought annuities, 58 percent of those aged 75 and older purchased VAs and 42 percent bought fixed annuities. Products like immediate variable annuities (IVAs) which allow customers to receive monthly payments immediately are increasingly being set up by providers to attract older investors.

Aetna Retirement Services unveiled an IVA geared primarily for older customers, said Aleida Herzog, product manager-fixed annuities and income products at the Hartford, Conn., insurer.

Well-invested traditional VAs have inflation-hedging qualities that retirees find appealing, Ms. Herzog said. She noted, for instance, that someone who invested $68,000 in a fixed annuity in 1980 would receive $140 monthly for life, whereas someone who purchased a VA in 1980 and invested in Aetna's growth and income fund would now be receiving $800 monthly.

Allmerica Financial, based in Worcester, Mass., currently manages $12 billion in VA assets and is developing its own IVA, said Mark Steinberg, managing director.

Allmerica uses a questionnaire and software program to determine a person's optimum asset allocation breakdown, Mr. Steinberg said. The company says virtually everybody, including older people, should have at least some equity exposure.

Source: Adapted from Joseph D'Allegro, "Insurers Say Seniors Should Keep Some Risk in Their Investments," *National Underwriter* (August 10, 1998): 7, 26. Used with permission.

change. Because annuities come in a variety of forms, they can be a useful part of a portfolio in each stage of a person's life, whether the purchaser's goal involves accumulating wealth or distributing a stream of income.

Risks Associated with Fixed and Equity-Indexed Annuities

As we mentioned in Chapter 3, fixed and equity-indexed annuities provide the security of guaranteed interest. However, the risk associated with changes in the economy and in the purchasing power of money affect both fixed and equity-indexed annuities. Three types of risk that we will discuss here are interest rate risk, inflation risk, and stagnant market risk.

Interest rate risk is the chance that unpredictable fluctuations in interest rates will jeopardize the opportunity to maximize the return on an investment. Because both fixed annuities and equity-indexed annuities are guaranteed to earn a specified interest rate, both types of annuities are subject to interest rate risk. For example, suppose Joachim Oliva puts $10,000 in a deferred fixed annuity paying 4 percent annual interest, with a withdrawal surrender charge for the first seven years. Three months after Mr. Oliva purchased the fixed annuity, interest rates began to rise rapidly, so that new fixed annuities were paying 6 percent interest. In this case, Mr. Oliva incurred the effects of interest rate risk. His annuity contract earned 4 percent interest, but if he had waited three months before purchasing the fixed annuity, he could have invested in a contract earning 6 percent.

Another form of risk is ***inflation risk***, the risk that the average level of prices for goods and services will increase during an investment period. During a period of inflation, if the value of an annuity does not increase at a rate equal to or greater than the inflation rate, the purchasing power of the dollars invested in the annuity will decrease. In other words, the contract owner will be unable to purchase as many goods and services as he had anticipated when he purchased the annuity. To help customers calculate how much money they will need in retirement, many financial services companies provide customers with illustrations of the possible growth of funds invested in 401(k) accounts. Indeed, a sum of $500,000 or more seems substantial when one considers today's prices. But suppose at retirement time a loaf of bread costs $15 and a new set of tires for a car costs $2,000. In such a scenario, inflation has adversely affected the value of the retirement account. For that reason, several financial services companies offer retirement planning software that includes inflation as a factor when customers calculate how much money they will need in retirement.

Interest rate risk and inflation risk affect both fixed and equity-indexed annuities. In addition, equity-indexed annuities can be affected by ***stagnant market risk***—the risk that the stock market will experience neither a significant gain nor a significant loss. In this situation, the equity-indexed annuity will still increase in value because of its interest rate guarantee. The contract owner, however, will not earn any excess interest credits, which are dependent on the performance of the stock market and are one of the attractive features of an equity-indexed annuity.

Risks Associated with Variable Annuities

You'll recall from our discussion in Chapter 4 that variable annuities provide some measure of protection against inflation risk. However, variable annuities are affected by ***market risk***—the risk associated with fluctuations in stock prices. In the case of a variable annuity, the greatest risk is not that the stock market will remain stagnant but that it will lose value, causing the variable annuity subaccount investments to lose principal or cash value as well. In fact, variable annuity contract owners face two risks: (1) that their subaccounts may not provide the desired returns and (2) that they may lose some of the principal they have invested in the contract.

The impact of market risk on variable annuities is most significant when the value of an annuity unit drops for contract owners who are receiving variable payouts. A significant drop in the value of an annuity unit will decrease payments, causing variable contract payees to receive less income than they expected to receive. However, investments in the stock market, including variable annuity stock subaccounts, historically have provided greater returns than more conservative investments such as bonds or fixed annuities.

INVESTMENT PRINCIPLES

As we noted earlier, an in-depth discussion of financial planning is beyond the scope of this text. However, understanding a few basic principles of investing can help a person better appreciate the value of investing in annuities.

The Time Value of Money

The *time value of money* is the concept that the value of a sum of money will change over time as the result of the effect of interest. The money you have today has a *present value (PV)*, the amount that you must invest today in order to accumulate a specified amount by a certain date. When that money is invested in an interest-bearing financial product—perhaps a savings account or a fixed annuity—that money also has a future value. A *future value (FV)* is an amount of money that you have invested plus what you will earn in interest over a certain period of time. The interest will be *compound interest*—interest earned on both the principal *and* the accumulated interest. Put simply, when money is invested properly, the time value of money operates so that an investment earns more money over time.

Because the time frames associated with retirement savings plans may be lengthy, the time value of money can have a tremendous impact on the growth of a person's investments. In other words, the amount of money that a person must save now—that is, the present value—is significantly smaller than the amount of money that a person will want to have at retirement—that is, the future value. Of course, the key is to begin saving as early as possible to allow the power of *compounding*—earning interest on both the principal *and* the accumulated interest—to dramatically increase the amount accumulated at retirement. Insight 5-2 provides a comparison of the effects of beginning a retirement savings program at age 25 versus age 35.

Dollar Cost Averaging

We discussed dollar cost averaging in Chapter 4 as a service insurers offer to their variable annuity customers. You will recall that this service allows contract owners to purchase a fixed dollar amount of accumulation units in a particular subaccount on a regular basis with the result that the average cost of those accumulation units is lower that it would be otherwise. With dollar cost averaging, the contract owner is able to purchase more accumulation units for his money.

INSIGHT 5.2

Saving for Retirement: Early vs. Late Start.

The sooner you start saving for retirement, the better, because the younger you are, the longer your money has a chance to compound. The best way to explain compounding is with an example. It's a story about two siblings—Anne and Jenny. Anne began contributing $100 a month to her 401(k) company retirement plan at the age of 25 and continued contributing until age 65.

Jenny, on the other hand, procrastinated. She never got around to investing for retirement until she was 35 years old (10 years after Anne). She began putting $100 a month away in her company 401(k) plan, and did so until she reached age 65. Both Anne and Jenny earned an average annual return of 8 percent on their accounts.

As you can see from the accompanying charts, both Anne and Jenny retired at age 65, but because Anne started saving 10 years earlier than Jenny, she earned $169,253 more in interest alone—and saved $181,253 more for her retirement. That's the benefit of compounding for you!

	Anne	Jenny
Starts Contributing at Age	25	35
Years of Contribution	40	30
Monthly Deposit	$100	$100
Total Contributions	$48,000	$36,000
Total Interest Earnings	$274,108	$104,855
Total Retirement Savings	$322,108	$140,855

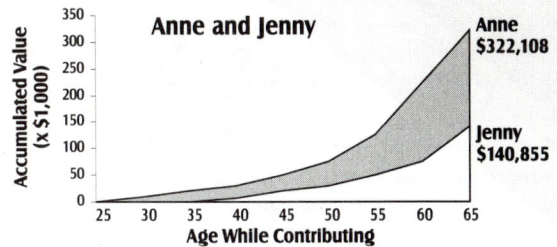

Anne and Jenny

Anne $322,108

Jenny $140,855

Accumulated Value (x $1,000) / Age While Contributing

Source: "How Early Should You Start?" *Manulife Financial,* http://www.manulife.com/usa/wwusdpen/early.htm (10 October 1998). Reprinted with permission.

Any investor can use the principle of dollar cost averaging to lower the average cost of share of a stock or a mutual fund, or the cost of an accumulation unit in a variable annuity. Figure 5-2 shows the results of using dollar cost averaging to purchase stocks

Diversification and Asset Allocation

In Chapter 4, we mentioned diversification in our discussion of choosing among a variable annuity's subaccounts. In a more general sense, when a person is choosing among a number of different investments, diversification allows him to minimize the risk of any one particular investment. One way to accomplish diversification is through asset allocation, which we also discussed in Chapter 4. If a person places all of his money in one type of investment and that investment loses its value, he will lose money. But, if he invests in several different types of investments, chances are that even if one does poorly, another will do well. The overall results will reduce risk and improve the return on the investments. In a sense, an investor who purchases one each of a fixed annuity, an equity-indexed annuity, and a variable annuity would have diversified her assets.

As part of a comprehensive strategy, a person can diversify a portfolio by including annuities along with stocks, bonds, savings accounts, or mutual funds. And a variable annuity contract itself can offer an opportunity for diversification because a contract owner can diversify his investments among subaccounts, thereby minimizing the risks from the poor performance of a few subaccounts.

FIGURE 5.2

The Effects of Dollar Cost Averaging over Time.

Say you began investing $100 per month in stocks on January 1, 1970—by 1980, after 10 years, the average price you paid for your units would have been a bit lower than the average unit price:

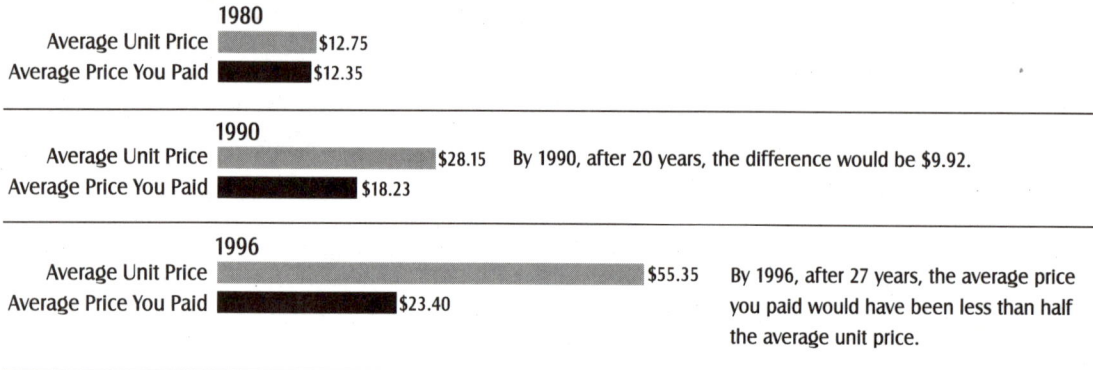

1980

Average Unit Price █████████ $12.75
Average Price You Paid ██████████ $12.35

1990

Average Unit Price █████████████ $28.15   By 1990, after 20 years, the difference would be $9.92.
Average Price You Paid ████████████ $18.23

1996

Average Unit Price █████████████████████████ $55.35   By 1996, after 27 years, the average price
Average Price You Paid █████████████ $23.40   you paid would have been less than half
the average unit price.

The chart above shows the actual results of investing $100 per month in the stocks of Standard & Poor's Composite Index of 500 Stocks from January 1, 1970, to December 31, 1996. At the end of the 27-year period, the average price you paid would have been $23.40, while the average unit price was $55.35.

ANNUITIES COMPARED TO OTHER FINANCIAL PRODUCTS

Before choosing to purchase any product, an investor should be aware of its relative advantages and disadvantages, including how the product compares with others in risk and return.

Annuities Compared to Savings Accounts and Certificates of Deposit

Many people who wish to minimize financial risk traditionally have preferred savings accounts and CDs as investment options. Individual accounts are insured up to $100,000 by the *Federal Deposit Insurance Corporation (FDIC)*—a U.S. federal agency that guarantees funds on deposit in member financial institutions. By investing in an FDIC-insured savings account or CD, investors can be sure that they will not lose the principal and any accrued interest up to $100,000. Even if a person has more than $100,000 to invest, he can ensure that the total amount is protected by opening more than one account.

A fixed annuity is the annuity product most comparable to a savings account or a CD. Compared to the interest rates paid on savings accounts and CDs, fixed annuity guaranteed interest rates are generally higher. In addition, a retiree who lives a very long life and chooses a type of life annuity potentially could receive annuity payments that far exceed the amount of money invested and accumulated in the fixed annuity. With an identical investment in a savings account or CD, the amount that the same retiree could withdraw over the same period of time—the principal, plus accrued interest—could be far less than the total of the fixed annuity payments.

One advantage of a savings account or CD over an annuity, however, is that the person has fewer restrictions on withdrawing money. The CD owner does have to wait for the CD's term to end, unless he is willing to pay a penalty to the bank for early withdrawal. But, as we discussed in Chapter 2, a fixed annuity contract owner's access to his money is governed by many annuity contract provisions. One common provision does allow contract owners to withdraw a certain percentage of the contract value each year without paying a surrender charge. However, as is the case with a withdrawal from a CD, the fixed annuity contract owner may have to pay surrender charges on some withdrawals that occur during the accumulation phase. In addition, the annuity contract owner may have to pay a federal tax penalty for most withdrawals made before age 59½. (We will cover tax penalties on annuities in Chapter 7.) CD withdrawals are not subject to such a tax penalty. Furthermore, if a payee is receiving annuity payments based on a straight life payout option, the early death of the annuitant might mean that the payee would not receive distributions equal to the principal invested in the annuity. Early death has no effect on the money held in a CD or savings account. On the other hand, as we have mentioned previously, an annuity contract owner can choose a number of different payout options, which would allow him or his beneficiaries to recover his investment in the contract or even give him a lifetime income that could exceed by many times his investment.

Annuities Compared to Mutual Funds

Variable annuities include subaccounts that function in much the same way as mutual funds, but variable annuities have a significant advantage in how they are taxed. The owner of a nonqualified annuity can transfer money from one subaccount of the variable annuity to another subaccount without taxation. The owner of shares in a mutual fund who chooses to transfer money into another mutual fund must first sell shares in the original fund, then buy shares in the new fund. If the owner sells the original mutual fund shares for more than he paid for them, he must pay taxes on the *capital gain*—the difference between his purchase price and selling price. Even if the owner leaves the money in the same mutual fund, if the fund itself sells shares of stocks that it owns for a profit or receives dividends, mutual fund shareholders must pay federal tax on their portion of the profit or dividends.

In a comparison of variable annuities and mutual funds, capital gains is an important topic. A possible disadvantage of variable annuities is that the federally taxable portion of payouts is taxed as ordinary income. Under current federal tax laws, money categorized as "ordinary income" is subject to higher tax rates than money classified by the Internal Revenue Code as "capital gains." However, the fact that an annuity's earnings accumulate tax deferred may increase its total value enough to more than offset the effect of its earnings being taxed at a higher rate than earnings from a mutual fund. The chart in Figure 5-3 compares the taxation of nonqualified individual annuities and mutual funds. We will discuss the tax issues associated with annuities in much greater detail in Chapter 7.

FIGURE 5.3

Taxation Comparisons.

After-Tax Annuities	Mutual Funds
Contributions: Contributions represent after-tax money and are tax-free when withdrawn.	**Contributions:** Contributions represent after-tax money and are tax-free when withdrawn.
Earnings: Accumulate tax deferred and are subject to the investor's ordinary income tax rate when withdrawn.	**Earnings:** Investment earnings are not tax deferred and are taxed in the calendar year in which they are earned. There are two categories of earnings: ordinary dividends and long-term capital gains. Ordinary dividends are distributions from the fund's net income, including interest, dividends, and "short-term" capital gains (gains from the sale of investments held twelve months or less). Ordinary dividends are taxed at the investor's regular income tax rate. Long-term capital gains are distributions from the sale of investments held more than twelve months and are taxed at a maximum rate of 20 percent.
Withdrawals: A single-sum withdrawal is treated as a withdrawal of investment earnings or interest and is taxable. Once all the earnings have been withdrawn, any other withdrawals are from the original contributions, which are not taxable since they've already been taxed.	**Withdrawals:** The taxation of withdrawals is based on the difference between the amount withdrawn or sold and the original cost of the mutual fund shares.
Early Withdrawals: Any withdrawals made before age 59$^{1}/_{2}$ are subject to the federal 10 percent early-withdrawal penalty tax.	**Early Withdrawals:** Mutual fund withdrawals are not subject to the federal 10 percent early-withdrawal penalty tax.
Transfers Between Accounts: Are not taxable.	**Transfers Between Accounts:** Exchanges from one mutual fund to another are taxable events and any gains will be taxed.

Source: TIAA-CREF, "After-Tax Investing," *The Participant* (August 1998): 16. Reprinted with permission.

Although variable annuities also include charges that could make them more expensive to purchase than comparable mutual funds, they do provide a benefit and they offer options that mutual funds do not: (1) a death benefit with some type of guarantee, (2) a fixed account option, and (3) a payout option, which allows the contract owner to receive regular payments.

Annuities Compared to Stocks and Bonds

Many investors purchase individual stocks and bonds directly. But people who prefer purchasing variable annuities, rather than picking individual stocks and bonds, may not have the time to do the research necessary to feel confident about their choices, may believe that professionals who manage variable annuity subaccounts can do a better job than they can, or feel that picking stocks and bonds themselves would be too risky.

Variable annuity purchasers pay a fee for the services of subaccount managers. An investor who picks her own stocks and bonds also would have to pay fees, of course, but, depending on the volume of shares purchased, those fees could be less than the fees the insurers charge. However, unless an investor has a very large sum of money to invest in stocks and bonds, he would be unable to achieve the kind of diversification available through purchasing a variable annuity, which offers multiple fund choices.

KEY TERMS AND CONCEPTS

certificate of deposit (CD)
interest rate risk
inflation risk
stagnant market risk
market risk
time value of money
present value (PV)
future value (FV)
compound interest
compounding
Federal Deposit Insurance Corporation (FDIC)
capital gain

CHAPTER 6

Individual and Group Annuities

After studying this chapter, you should be able to

◆ Describe how people use individual non-qualified annuities to save for retirement, manage lump sum cash distributions, and pay for the cost of a college education

◆ Explain how individual nonqualified annuities differ from IRAs

◆ Discuss the features that distinguish traditional IRAs, Roth IRAs, and education IRAs

◆ Describe how ERISA regulations affect employer-sponsored retirement plans in the United States

◆ Explain the difference between a qualified retirement plan and a nonqualified retirement plan

◆ List and describe the types of retirement plans most commonly offered by employers in the United States

As you know from our discussion so far, insurers offer several types of annuity products—fixed, equity-indexed, variable, and market value adjusted—and they sell these products in both individual and group markets. And, as we have noted, investors purchase annuities to satisfy a variety of financial objectives. In this chapter, we will discuss the ways that individual nonqualified annuities are used as retirement savings instruments and how they can be used to meet other personal financial goals. We will also look at employer-sponsored retirement plans and discuss how both individual and group annuity contracts can be used to fund these plans.

INDIVIDUAL NONQUALIFIED ANNUITIES

Any investor—whether a natural person or a legal entity, such as a trust or corporation—can purchase an individual nonqualified annuity. Remember from our discussion in Chapter 1 that only annuities used to accumulate or distribute money from certain qualified plans are considered qualified annuities—all other annuities are referred to as nonqualified annuities. Later in this chapter, we will discuss the use of both qualified

and nonqualified annuities to fund group retirement plans; however, in this section we will limit our discussion to the purchase of individual nonqualified annuities by natural persons.

Natural persons—people—purchase individual nonqualified annuities for a number of reasons, including (1) to save for retirement, (2) to manage a lump sum cash distribution from a retirement plan, or other source, and (3) to pay for the cost of a college education. Let's take a closer look now at how nonqualified annuities can help investors meet these financial objectives.

Retirement Savings

Accumulating assets for retirement is perhaps the most common reason that people purchase individual nonqualified annuities. Individual nonqualified annuities are attractive retirement savings vehicles for investors because (1) they allow investors to make regular contributions over time, (2) all earnings accumulate on a tax-deferred basis (for investors in the United States), and (3) accumulated money can be used to provide a monthly income at retirement. Any investor—whether or not he has any income from employment—can purchase an individual nonqualified annuity and realize the benefits of tax-deferred savings. However, people with earned income can take advantage of additional opportunities to accumulate money for retirement. To encourage workers to save for retirement, U.S. and Canadian federal tax laws contain provisions giving certain tax benefits to employed persons who deposit money in designated retirement savings plans. Let's take a closer look at these plans.

Individual Retirement Arrangements

In the United States, an **individual retirement arrangement (IRA)**, also known as an *individual retirement account* or *individual retirement annuity*, is an arrangement that allows people with earned income to deposit a portion of that income in a tax-deferred savings plan. An IRA is set up by a sponsoring financial institution, such as an insurance company, a bank, or an investment company. The sponsoring institution manages the account and invests the IRA contributions at the owner's direction. IRA contributions can be placed in bank savings accounts, mutual funds, or any of several other types of investments, including annuities.

Under current tax laws in the United States, people who meet certain eligibility requirements can contribute a portion of their earned income each year—up to a specified maximum—to an IRA. (In Chapter 7, we will discuss how Canadian laws allow individuals to establish retirement accounts similar to IRAs.) Eligible investors can choose to deposit money into a traditional IRA or a Roth IRA. Some or all of the amount deposited into a *traditional IRA* can be deducted from the investor's taxable income. A person's (1) gross income, (2) tax filing status, and (3) coverage under an employer-sponsored retirement plan determine the portion of the IRA contribution that is deductible from taxable income. Because some investors are able to deduct their IRA contributions, it is accurate to call that money "tax-qualified," but it is important to note that IRAs are not qualified plans as defined by the Internal Revenue Code. Taxes on the deductible portion of the IRA contributions and all investment earnings are deferred until money is withdrawn from the account.

In a *Roth IRA*, no portion of account contributions is deductible from the investor's taxable income. However, if certain criteria are met, both the contributions to the account and all investment earnings generated from the contributions can be withdrawn from a Roth IRA on a tax-free basis.

Although an investor can make withdrawals from a traditional IRA or Roth IRA at any time, if she makes withdrawals before she reaches age 59½, in most cases, she will have to pay a 10 percent tax penalty in addition to paying any income tax due on the withdrawal. The purpose of the tax penalty on early withdrawals is to encourage investors to wait until they reach retirement age to use the money held in an IRA. Tax penalties are also imposed on an investor who fails to begin making withdrawals from a traditional IRA by the time she reaches age 70½. However, no comparable tax penalty is imposed if the investor fails to make withdrawals from a Roth IRA by the time she reaches age 70½.

Individual Nonqualified Annuities and IRAs

As we have noted, people use individual nonqualified annuities and IRAs to save for retirement. As you know, both types of financial instruments provide certain tax advantages for the investor, and both types of financial instruments impose penalties on early withdrawals to encourage people to hold money in these accounts until retirement. However, despite these similarities, significant differences exist between individual nonqualified annuities and IRAs.

First, no portion of premiums used to purchase an individual nonqualified annuity outside of an IRA is tax-deductible. However, some or all of the contributions made to a traditional IRA may be tax-deductible. In addition, contributions to an individual nonqualified annuity are not restricted—as they are with an IRA—to people who have earned income or their spouses. Further, non-IRA contributions to an individual nonqualified annuity typically can be in any amount with no maximum contribution limits. But, traditional IRA contributions are limited by law to 100 percent of a person's earned income or $2,000 annually, whichever is less. Roth IRA contributions are subject to even further limitations, depending on the income level of the investor. Finally, while an individual nonqualified annuity contract may specify a maximum age at which payouts must begin—a provision that is usually dictated by state laws—this age is typically higher than the maximum age of 70½ allowed under a traditional IRA. Figure 6-1 compares traditional IRAs, Roth IRAs, and individual non-qualified annuities. Note that the regulations governing IRAs apply whether the IRA contributions are invested in an annuity or some other investment vehicle, such as a mutual fund.

Lump Sum Distributions

In addition to functioning as retirement savings vehicles, individual annuities can be used to manage lump sum distributions from employer-sponsored retirement plans or other lump sum cash distributions. Distributions from an employer-sponsored retirement plan are payable to an eligible employee either upon separation of employment or at retirement. Depending on the terms of the plan and the employee's tax circumstances at the time benefits are payable, she may choose to receive a lump sum. After she has paid taxes on the lump sum, she can then invest the remainder in an individual nonqualified annuity to provide a monthly income payment during her retirement. Alternately, depending on her age, she can "roll over" the entire sum into an IRA, so that the taxes due on the disbursed amount can be deferred. Note that only certain disbursements from designated individual and employer-sponsored retirement accounts can be "rolled over" into an IRA.

FIGURE 6.1

A Comparison of Traditional IRAs, Roth IRAs, and Individual Nonqualified Annuities (Non-IRA).

	Traditional IRA	Roth IRA	Individual Nonqualified Annuity (Non-IRA)
Earned Income Requirements	YES	YES	NO
Contributions Deductible from Taxable Income	YES *Deductible amount determined by income*	NO	NO
Investment Earnings Tax-Deferred	YES	YES *Tax free after 5 years*	YES
Tax Penalties for Early Withdrawal*	YES	YES	YES
Maximum Age for Payouts	YES *70½*	NO	YES *As specified in the contract*
Contribution Limits	YES *$2,000 annually, or 100% of earned income*	YES *$2,000 annually, subject to income eligibility limits*	NO *Unless specified in contract*

*Penalties may be waived under certain circumstances.

Other situations in which an investor may wish to deposit a lump sum in an annuity are (1) upon receipt of an inheritance or insurance settlement, (2) after selling a home or a business, or (3) when receiving a large cash bonus or gift.

Education Funding

Finally, some investors purchase individual annuities to pay for future higher education costs for a child or grandchild. Traditional IRAs, Roth IRAs, and individual nonqualified annuities can be used to pay certain higher education costs; however, a special investment option is available for investors who want to accumulate money for this purpose. An *education IRA* is a special type of IRA that allows the owner to make withdrawals prior to age 59½ without penalty, if he uses the money to pay for certain qualifying education costs. Like traditional and Roth IRAs, education IRA contributions can be placed in any of several types of investments, including annuities. Contributions to an education IRA are not tax-deductible, and maximum annual contribution limits are considerably lower than those allowed for traditional and Roth IRAs. However, both the contributions to the account and all investment earnings generated from the contributions can be withdrawn on a tax-free basis if used to pay for qualifying education costs.

In some instances, investors can make penalty-free withdrawals from a traditional IRA, a Roth IRA, or an individual nonqualified annuity to cover certain qualifying education costs. However, unlike money withdrawn from an education IRA, money withdrawn from a traditional IRA, a Roth IRA, or an individual nonqualified annuity may be subject to taxation.

GROUP RETIREMENT PLANS AND ANNUITIES

In addition to providing incentives for workers to save for retirement, the U.S. and Canadian federal governments also offer incentives for employers to set up retirement plans for their employees. Federal tax laws in the United States and Canada provide certain economic benefits to *plan sponsors*—employers that establish private retirement plans—and *plan participants*—employees who are covered by these private retirement plans. In Chapter 7, we will discuss the favorable tax treatment given to employer and employee contributions to certain types of retirement plans in the United States and Canada. As with individual retirement plans, group retirement plan contributions can be placed in a variety of investments—including annuities.

Most employer-employee group retirement plans in the United States must comply with the federal Employee Retirement Income Security Act (ERISA) and other federal regulations, which provide rules and requirements for employee benefit and retirement plans. ERISA contains provisions for determining if an employee benefit or retirement plan is qualified or nonqualified. Qualified plans must meet specific requirements included in U.S. Internal Revenue Code Section 401(a):

◆ **Participation.** In order to participate in the plan, an employee cannot be required to complete a period of service beyond the later of one year or the employee's attainment of age 21. Thus, the minimum age requirement for participation in the plan cannot be more than 21 *and* employees who meet the age requirement must be eligible to participate after completing one year of employment. However, if an employee will be fully vested in the plan after two years of service, the plan can impose a minimum service requirement of two years.

◆ **Vesting.** A participant's interest in a plan is vested when he is entitled to receive partial or full benefits under the plan even if he no longer works for the sponsoring employer at the time of his retirement. A plan participant's right to receive benefits funded by employer contributions must vest within a specified period after the participant becomes eligible to join the plan. A plan participant's right to receive benefits funded by his own contributions must vest immediately.

◆ **Nondiscrimination.** The plan cannot discriminate in favor of highly paid employees.

◆ **Distribution.** The plan must contain specific provisions regarding when benefits will begin to be paid and what, if any, benefits will be payable upon the death of the plan participant.

◆ **Investments.** To ensure the safety of retirement benefits, a variety of regulations govern the ways insurers and other financial services providers must invest retirement plan assets.

◆ **Reporting.** The plan sponsor is required to provide periodic reports about the plan's provisions and performance to governmental agencies and to plan participants.

In Canada, the federal government and all the provinces have each enacted a *Pension Benefits Act* that governs the terms and operation of private retirement plans. This legislation requires employers to register these plans with a specified government agency. In order to qualify for registration, the plan must comply with a number of requirements—which vary from province to province—similar to the requirements that ERISA imposes on qualified plans in the United States. However, unlike the requirements contained in ERISA, Canadian legislation requires that all registered plan benefits be portable so that they can be moved from one registered plan to another.

Qualified Retirement Plans

Recall from Chapter 1 that an employee benefit plan—such as a retirement plan—that satisfies legal requirements to receive certain federal tax benefits is known as a qualified plan in the United States. In Canada, such a plan is known as a *registered pension plan (RPP)*. A nonqualified plan does not meet the same legal requirements as does a qualified plan and therefore does not receive the same federal tax benefits. Remember too, that an annuity is "qualified" only when it is purchased as part of a qualified plan.

When an employer establishes a qualified retirement plan, the employer also appoints a *plan trustee*, who holds legal title to the retirement plan assets on behalf of the plan participants. Typically, the trustee is responsible for administering and maintaining plan assets. If an employer funds a retirement plan with an annuity, the trustee can invest plan assets either in a group annuity contract covering all participants or individual annuity contracts for each participant. For administrative purposes, group annuities are most commonly used in plans covering large numbers of employees. When the plan trustee purchases a group annuity, the plan trustee is the owner of the group contract. The plan trustee receives a master contract and participating employees receive a certificate when they enroll in the plan. The terms of the group annuity contract control the trustee's investment of the plan's assets. On the other hand, when the trustee purchases individual annuities, a separate contract is issued for each plan participant. These individual contracts are normally issued to and owned by the plan trustee. As with group annuity contracts, the terms of the individual annuity contract control how the trustee can invest plan assets in the annuity.

Let's take a closer look now at the three most common types of employer-sponsored qualified retirement plans: (1) pension plans, (2) profit sharing plans, and (3) retirement savings plans.

Pension Plans

The term *pension plan* can have a variety of meanings. For the purposes of our classification system, a **pension plan** is an agreement under which an employer establishes a plan to provide its employees with a lifetime monthly income benefit that begins at retirement. The employer obligates itself to fund, in advance, at least a portion of the pension plan's promised benefits. Although employers can select from various types of pension plans, each qualified pension plan can be categorized as either a defined benefit plan or a defined contribution plan.

A **defined benefit plan** is a type of pension plan that specifies the amount of benefit—based on the employee's income, years of service, or both income and year's of service—a participant will receive at retirement. The retirement benefit is usually described in terms of a monthly annuity, and the plan sponsor is obligated to deposit enough assets into the plan to provide the promised benefits. An actuary determines the amount of contributions the employer needs to make to fund the plan by estimating employee mortality, turnover, future salaries, administrative expenses, and plan investment earnings. For investment purposes, the plan trustee typically pools into one account the total contributions an employer makes on behalf of all plan participants. As plan participants retire, the plan trustee distributes the retirement plan benefits in accordance with the plan's provisions.

A **defined contribution plan**, also known as a *money purchase plan*, is a type of pension plan that specifies the annual contribution the employer will deposit into the plan on behalf of each plan participant. Usually, this contribution is a specified percentage of the participant's salary or wages. The plan trustee can allocate employer contributions to individual accounts for each participant or pool contributions into one account with relative percentages assigned to each participant. The plan trustee or plan administrator provides record keeping services so that individual accounts can be maintained within a group annuity. Plan contributions are invested and accumulated on behalf of each plan participant. When a plan participant retires, the total amount allocated to that person is available either in a lump sum or in the form of a monthly annuity, depending on the provisions of the plan. The amount of the annuity payment that each retiree receives depends upon the amount that has accumulated in the account during his working years. Thus, although the amount of money going into the plan is clearly specified, the exact amount of the payment is not known until the retiree begins to receive payments.

In recent years, plan sponsors have tended to establish pension plans as defined contribution plans rather than as defined benefit plans. The reasons behind this trend include the tendency of employees to change jobs more frequently than was the case in the past and the costs required to fund a pension plan. When an employer establishes a defined contribution plan, it knows in advance what the cost will be to fund the plan each year. By contrast, an employer that is funding a defined benefit plan must rely on actuarial estimates of what the cost will be to fund the plan each year. In addition, ERISA imposes more complex requirements on defined benefit plans than it imposes on defined contribution plans.

Profit Sharing Plans

A **profit sharing plan** that qualifies for favorable tax treatment is typically a type of employer-sponsored retirement plan that is funded primarily by employer contributions payable from, and usually based on, the employer's profits. A qualified profit sharing plan functions in most respects like a defined contribution pension plan. However, the employer does not determine the amount of the contributions in advance and so the contribution amount can change from year to year. In fact, in some years, the employer may not make any contributions. By contrast, an employer must make contributions to a qualified *pension plan* every year, in accordance with a formula stated in the plan.

Retirement Savings Plans

Retirement savings plans are another form of qualified plan that employers in the United States can use to provide retirement benefits to their employees. One of the most common plans offered by employers is the **401(k) plan**, an arrangement that allows both employers and employees to make contributions to a tax-deferred retirement savings plan established for the benefit of employees. The name *401(k)* refers to the section of the U.S. Internal Revenue Code that permits the creation of these plans. Under a 401(k) plan, the employer establishes an account for each participant and all contributions made on behalf of the participant are credited to his account. An employee is allowed to contribute a percentage of his earned income—up to a specified maximum—to the plan each year. An employer is not obligated to make contributions to an employee's 401(k) account. If the employer does make a contribution, the amount usually is equal to the amount contributed by the employee or is a percentage of that amount, subject to a specified maximum. The amount of an employer's contribution to a 401(k) plan is deductible from the employer's current taxable income.

To provide an incentive for employees to participate in 401(k) retirement savings plans, U.S. federal tax laws allow employees to contribute money to the plan—subject to certain limitations—on a pre-tax basis. In other words, when an employee contributes to a 401(k) plan, the amount of the contribution is not included in the employee's current gross taxable income. Instead, contributions are taxed upon withdrawal from the 401(k) plan. In addition, taxes on employer contributions to the plan and all earnings from investments in the plan are deferred until money is withdrawn from the plan. Premature disbursements from the plan—prior to age 59½—usually are subject to a federal tax penalty. However, depending on plan guidelines, participants may be eligible to take penalty-free loans on 401(k) balances. We will discuss loans from 401(k) plans in Chapter 7.

401(k) plans are usually established for employees of for-profit organizations. The U.S. Internal Revenue Code also includes federal tax benefits for retirement savings plans established for employees of not-for-profit organizations and employees of both state and local governments. While these plans do not meet the definition of "qualified" as specified in the IRC, they offer many of the same tax advantages as qualified plans. A **403(b) plan** is an arrangement that allows not-for-profit employers and their employees to make contributions to a tax-deferred retirement savings plan established for the benefit of employees. A **457 plan** is an arrangement that allows state and local governments and their employees to make contributions to a tax-deferred retirement savings plan established for the benefit of employees. Like the 401(k) plan, 403(b) and 457 plans are named for the sections of the U.S. Internal Revenue Code that permit the respective plan's creation. As with 401(k) plans, participants in 403(b) plans and 457 plans are allowed to make pre-tax contributions from their income—up to specified limits—and all investment earnings accumulate on a tax-deferred basis. The regulations governing 403(b) and 457 employer contributions differ somewhat from those governing employer contributions to 401(k) plans. However, regulations regarding account withdrawals are similar to those pertaining to 401(k) plans.

Participants in 401(k), 403(b), and 457 retirement savings plans can place their contributions in a variety of investment vehicles, including annuities. In fact, participants in 403(b) plans and employees of certain tax-exempt organizations are eligible to invest in a special type of annuity known as a Tax Sheltered Annuity. A **Tax Sheltered Annuity (TSA)** is a retirement annuity sold only to public school teachers and employees of hospitals, colleges, and other organizations offering qualified retirement plans under section 403(b) of the U.S. Internal Revenue Code. As with the other retirement savings plans we have discussed, TSAs are subject to regulations regarding maximum contribution limits, premature withdrawals, and loans against account balances. These regulations, however, are slightly different than those that apply to annuities purchased as part of a 401(k) or 457 plan.

Keogh Plans

Another type of retirement savings plan offering special tax advantages for investors in the United States is the **Keogh plan**, an arrangement that allows self-employed persons to deposit a portion of their income earned from self-employment in a tax-deferred savings plan. A Keogh plan is set up by a sponsoring financial institution, such as an insurance company, a bank, or an investment company. The sponsoring financial institution manages the Keogh plan and invests plan contributions at the owner's direction.

Plan contributions can be placed in any of several types of investments, including annuities.

The owner of a Keogh plan can deposit a portion of her annual earned income from self-employment—up to a specified maximum—into the account each year. She can then deduct this amount from her taxable income. The maximum annual contribution allowed under a Keogh plan is the lesser of 25 percent of annual income or $30,000. In addition, investment earnings are not taxable until they are withdrawn from the account.

Because contributions are tax-deductible and investment earnings are tax-deferred, all withdrawals from a Keogh plan are taxable as income. However, the investor may have to pay federal tax penalties on withdrawals if she fails to meet certain requirements. These withdrawal penalties are designed to encourage people to use money held in a Keogh plan for retirement.

Simplified Employee Pension Plans

Because of the complexity of the laws governing retirement plan administration and the costs associated with establishing a retirement plan, many employers—especially small employers—are unable to offer pension and other retirement savings benefits to their employees. In order to make retirement plans more available to the employees of these businesses, U.S. federal tax laws provide tax benefits for qualified employer-sponsored plans known as simplified employee pension plans. Under a *simplified employee pension (SEP) plan*, an employer establishes and makes contributions into an IRA for each participating employee. Generally, participating employees do not make contributions to the plan. The amount of an employer's contribution to a SEP plan, subject to designated maximums, is deductible as a business expense from the employer's taxable income. Also, the amount of this contribution is excluded from the employee's taxable income. The maximum deductible amount that can be contributed to a SEP IRA is considerably higher than the maximum deductible amount permitted with an individually established IRA. Because of the higher deductible amounts available through a SEP plan, many self-employed people also establish SEP IRAs.

Typically, employers establish SEP plans because they are easy to administer and they reduce the amount of paperwork normally associated with establishing a qualified pension plan or other type of qualified retirement savings plan. Nevertheless, the employer must ensure that the plan meets various legal requirements concerning the eligible employees who the plan must cover and the contribution amounts that the employer can make on behalf of specific classes of employees.

Savings Incentive Match Plan for Employees

For small business owners in the United States, two alternatives to the retirement savings plans we have discussed are the Savings Incentive Match

Plan for Employees (SIMPLE) IRA and the Savings Incentive Match Plan for Employees (SIMPLE) 401(k). The *Savings Incentive Match Plan for Employees (SIMPLE) IRA* is a special arrangement whereby an employer with 100 or fewer employees can establish a simplified retirement savings plan for employees. Under the plan, both the employer and employee can make tax-deductible contributions—up to specified maximums—to an IRA the employer has established for the employee. Like a traditional or Roth IRA, investment earnings accumulate on a tax-deferred basis. However, the maximum annual contribution allowed under a SIMPLE IRA is considerably higher than that allowed for a traditional or Roth IRA. In most other respects, a SIMPLE IRA is subject to the same general regulations as a traditional or Roth IRA.

The *Savings Incentive Match Plan for Employees (SIMPLE) 401(k)* is a special arrangement whereby an employer with 100 or fewer employees can establish a simplified 401(k) retirement savings plan for employees. The SIMPLE 401(k) plan functions in much the same way as a regular 401(k) plan—both the employer and the employee can make contributions to the plan up to a specified maximum. Employer contributions to the plan are deductible from the employer's current taxable income, employee contributions are made on a pre-tax basis, and all earnings on investments held in the account accumulate on a tax-deferred basis. However, a SIMPLE 401(k) does not require the same level of administrative support needed to manage a regular 401(k) plan. As with SEP plans and SIMPLE IRA plans, a SIMPLE 401(k) plan allows an employer to make contributions to an employee's retirement savings without incurring the higher costs often associated with other types of qualified pension and retirement plans. Insight 6-1 offers a closer look at SIMPLE plans.

Nonqualified Retirement Plans

Because qualified retirement plans receive favorable tax treatment, many employers have established them. Nevertheless, in some situations, employers provide other means for employees to save for retirement that do not qualify for all the tax benefits available to qualified plans. An employer can establish a nonqualified plan either (1) as an alternative to establishing a qualified plan or (2) to supplement an existing qualified plan.

The primary advantage to an employer of establishing a nonqualified retirement plan is that the employer is relieved from complying with much of the complex legislation and stringent requirements that govern qualified plans. For example, an employer that establishes a nonqualified plan can provide additional benefits to certain classes of employees, such as highly paid executives, who cannot receive special treatment under a qualified plan. As with qualified plans, employer and employee contributions to a nonqualified plan can be placed in a variety of investments, including annuities.

INSIGHT 6.1

Whatever Happened to SIMPLE Plans?

The Savings Incentive Match Plans for Employees of Small Employers (SIMPLE) became effective January 1, 1997, under the 1996 Small Business Jobs Protection Act.

When the SIMPLE IRA plan was first introduced, it seemed ideal for many small employers. After all, only 21 percent of companies with fewer than 100 employees had 401(k) plans, according to a 1997 study by Access Research (see *National Underwriter*, July 20, 1998). This low number is not surprising, considering the $1,500 to $2,000 annual administrative costs that even small 401(k) plans had to pay. Such costs posed too great a burden for small employers, in view of the small number of participants involved.

However, to date, the response to the SIMPLE concept from many insurance companies and other vendors has been less than enthusiastic.

In September 1998, The Advantage Group conducted an informal survey of 25 large insurance companies, asking if they were targeting the SIMPLE IRA market. Over three-quarters of the 25 companies which answered said they either didn't offer SIMPLE plans or didn't market them.

Why not? Some companies said they were allocating resources to Roth IRA marketing. Others said that they felt SIMPLE plans were a good idea, but they didn't feel there was a market for them yet.

While SIMPLE IRAs are on hold at a number of insurers, some carriers do believe in their potential.

One large insurer had over 1,000 SIMPLE IRA plans on the books with over 11,000 participants, as of mid-1998. The company's core market is closely held businesses typically with 10 or fewer employees. This insurer says

small employers that can't afford the administrative costs of 401(k) plans are good candidates for SIMPLE IRA plans.

Another large insurer had opened over 600 SIMPLE IRA plans, as of mid-1998. It reports implementing plans ranging in size from sole proprietors to companies with as many as 65 employees. The plans are often used in businesses where owners are expecting little or no employee contributions or where owner contributions are restricted in an existing plan. Company officials say plans are also used by small tax-exempt employers, start-up firms, and companies with current top-heavy plans.

Are SIMPLE plans simply in the early stages of a learning curve that will see explosive growth in the future, or are they a pension alternative that is too restrictive to flourish? We will need to look to the future for the answers.

Source: Adapted from Jack Marrion, "Whatever Happened to the SIMPLE Plans?" *National Underwriter* (September 28, 1998): 8, 22. Used with permission.

KEY TERMS AND CONCEPTS

individual retirement arrangement (IRA)
plan sponsors
plan participants
Pension Benefits Act
registered pension plan (RPP)
plan trustee
pension plan
defined benefit plan
defined contribution plan
profit sharing plan
401(k) plan
403(b) plan
457 plan
Tax Sheltered Annuity (TSA)
Keogh plan
simplified employee pension (SEP) plan
Savings Incentive Match Plan for Employees (SIMPLE) IRA
Savings Incentive Match Plan for Employees (SIMPLE) 401(k)

CHAPTER 7

Taxation of Annuities

After studying this chapter, you should be able to

◆ Discuss the differences between the U.S. tax treatment of annuity premiums deposited into nonqualified annuities and into qualified annuities

◆ Describe the U.S. income tax treatment of withdrawals, surrenders, and distributions

◆ Explain how annuities are treated with regard to estate taxes in the United States

◆ Describe U.S. tax penalties that affect annuity withdrawals

◆ Describe Section 1035 exchanges

◆ Describe rollovers

◆ Discuss the tax treatment of annuities in Canada

In the United States, annuities receive favorable treatment under federal tax regulations. We will explore the tax treatment of annuities by discussing the impact that income taxes, penalty taxes, and estate taxes have on annuities, contract owners, and beneficiaries. We will also discuss the tax treatment of exchanges of nonqualified annuity contracts and rollovers of qualified annuity contracts.

Because the United States affords individual annuities a more favorable tax status than does Canada, most of the chapter will be devoted to the tax treatment of annuities within the United States. However, we will also briefly cover some aspects of annuity tax treatment in Canada.

You will recall from our discussions in previous chapters that annuities are either qualified or nonqualified depending upon whether or not they meet certain criteria specified in the Internal Revenue Code (IRC) and the Employee Retirement Income Security Act (ERISA). Several hundred pages of detailed regulations related to annuities have been generated from the provisions that the IRC and ERISA contain. We will not go into great detail or even specify which IRC or ERISA provision has resulted in a particular regulation, but we will highlight the most important information on taxation of annuities. See Figure 7-1 for a brief description of the sources of taxation requirements for annuities.

INCOME TAXES

Depending upon the type of annuity contract purchased, at some point in time a contract owner or plan participant very likely will have to pay *income tax*—a tax that is levied on income that a person or business earns—on an annuity contract's earnings. (As we discussed in Chapter 6, one exception is the Roth IRA, which is purchased with after-tax dollars and whose earnings can be withdrawn tax-free.) He may also pay income tax when he withdraws money that includes any deposits that he made with *before-tax dollars*, that is, money that has not been taxed previously. Of course, a number of different variables affect whether a person pays income tax on his income, including any payments or withdrawals from an annuity contract.

Tax Deferral on Investment Income

Like other types of income, earnings on the money invested in an annuity contract are subject

---

FIGURE 7.1

Sources of Taxation Requirements for Annuities.

Internal Revenue Code

The federal tax code of the United States is contained in the Internal Revenue Code, which spells out various tax laws and rulings that cover income, estate, gift, employment, and excise taxes. Some of the sections relate specifically to annuities and other insurance and retirement products. For example, Section 72 contains information specific to annuities and their tax treatment. Section 401 covers employer-sponsored retirement plans. Section 403 covers tax-sheltered annuities for certain types of nonprofit organizations. Section 408 includes information specific to Individual Retirement Annuities. Section 1035 deals with nontaxable exchanges of insurance policies and annuity contracts.

ERISA

In the United States, the majority of pension plan legislation has been provided by the Employee Retirement Income Security Act (ERISA) of 1974. ERISA established standards relating to the rights of pension plan participants, investment standards for plan assets, and the disclosure and reporting of plan provisions and funding.

---

to income taxes. (The Roth IRA is an exception.) However, an annuity provides a way for a person to earn money over time and to defer paying taxes on those earnings. Ownership of an annuity does not totally exempt the contract owner from paying income taxes on the annuity's income, but allows him to postpone the payment of those income taxes until he either makes a withdrawal from the annuity account or begins to receive annuity payments.

For example, suppose Milos Fortias purchases a deferred annuity at age 40, but waits 20 years before he begins to receive annuity payments. Although the annuity contract earns investment income for 20 years, Mr. Fortias does not have to pay taxes on this income until he begins receiving annuity payments at age 60, assuming he makes no withdrawals during the 20-year period.

Many people purchase annuities to take advantage of this deferred income tax treatment. However, only persons are eligible for this special tax treatment. Corporations, trusts, and other legal entities that own annuities usually must pay income taxes on annuity income each year. Exceptions to this requirement include some types of trusts held for the benefit of a natural person. In these cases, the income tax on the annuity earnings is deferred until the annuity payments begin.

Deductibility of Premium Payments for the Plan Participant

In some cases, annuity premiums also receive favorable income tax treatment. For example, a plan participant in certain types of qualified retirement plans can deduct the premiums that he pays into the annuity—up to a stated maximum—from his income each year, reducing his taxable income. Thus, the qualified retirement plan participant gets two tax breaks: (1) he avoids paying income tax on the amount of his income that he uses to pay the annuity premiums and (2) he is not taxed on the earnings that the annuity accumulates during the year until he makes a withdrawal or begins to receive annuity payments.

However, only those annuities that are part of certain types of employer-sponsored qualified retirement plans are afforded this tax treatment. You'll recall that examples of employer-sponsored qualified retirement plans include retirement savings plans such as 401(k) or 403(b) plans, pension plans, and profit-sharing plans. Figure 7-2 provides a brief review of some employer-sponsored qualified retirement plans.

FIGURE 7.2

Types of Employer-Sponsored Qualified Retirement Plans.

Retirement Savings Plans

401(k) Plan. A retirement plan established by an employer that enables employees to make pretax contributions by salary reduction agreements. Thus, the employee's contributions are deductible from the employee's taxable income.

403(b) Plan. A type of retirement plan established for employees by certain tax-exempt organizations and public schools. The employer can contribute to the employee's retirement annuity policy and the contributions will be deductible from the employee's gross income.

Pension Plan

An agreement under which an employer establishes a plan to provide its employees with a lifetime monthly income benefit that begins at their retirement. Employees must meet certain age and service requirements to qualify.

Profit Sharing Plan

A type of employer-sponsored savings plan that is funded primarily by contributions payable from the employer's profits. Because contributions are voluntary, the employer does not have to contribute to the plan.

Another tax-related advantage of qualified annuities is that the employee's taxable income base may be lower when she begins to receive annuity payments. For most people, annual income is higher during working years and lower in retirement. Thus, the withdrawals or payments from the annuity presumably will be taxed at a lower rate than the tax rate that would have been paid on those amounts during the employee's working years.

Deductibility of Premium Payments for Owners of IRAs and Nonqualified Annuities

Several factors affect whether premiums paid into an individual annuity are deductible. You'll recall from our discussion of traditional IRAs that a person may be able to deduct all or a portion of her contributions from her federally taxable income, but may not deduct contributions to a Roth IRA. However, when a contract owner withdraws money that has not been taxed from a traditional IRA, she then pays income tax on the amount of the withdrawal. On the other hand, withdrawals of contributions and earnings from a Roth IRA that meet certain criteria are tax-free.

As we mentioned earlier in this chapter, nonqualified annuities do not have the same tax advantages that qualified annuities do. Premium payments for nonqualified annuities are nondeductible—that is, the contract owner pays income taxes on his earned income and then uses *after-tax dollars*—money after taxes have been paid on it—to purchase the annuity. Because the contract owner pays premiums with after-tax dollars, no governmental restrictions exist on how much a person can contribute to a nonqualified annuity. However, as we discussed in Chapter 6, limits do exist on the dollar amount that a plan participant can contribute to a 401(k) or 403(b) plan each year.

Income earned within the nonqualified annuity, however, does accumulate on a tax-deferred basis. Whether the owner later surrenders the nonqualified annuity contract, makes a withdrawal, or receives annuity payments, the amount of money that he contributed—often called the *tax cost basis*—will not be subject to taxation because it has already been taxed.

Deductibility of Premium Payments for Sponsors of Qualified Retirement Plans

In Chapter 6 we discussed a number of different group retirement plans sponsored by employers. You will recall that the federal income tax laws in the United States contain economic incentives for retirement plan sponsors as well as for participants in these plans.

Although the Internal Revenue Service does not require employers in the United States to obtain advance approval of their retirement plans in order to receive favorable tax treatment, most employers choose to do so to ensure that their plans meet the qualified plan requirements. As we mentioned earlier in this chapter, the majority of retirement plan legislation in the United States is found in ERISA and in subsequent tax legislation. ERISA amended virtually all federal tax laws that applied to qualified retirement plans. Although tax laws tend to be amended fairly frequently, in Figure 7-3 we have included a summary of the current federal income tax treatment of employee and employer contributions to and earnings from a qualified retirement plan.

FIGURE 7.3

Federal Income Tax Treatment of Qualified Retirement Contributions and Earnings.

◆ Within stated limits, contributions an employer makes to a qualified plan on behalf of employees are deductible by the employer from current taxable income. These contributions are considered to be a business expense.

◆ Contributions an employer makes to a qualified plan on an employee's behalf are not considered to be part of the employee's current taxable income. Instead, the plan participant pays income taxes on the value of the employer's contributions (adding any gains and subtracting any losses) when he actually receives payments from the plan.

◆ The investment earnings on plan contributions—whether the employer or the employee makes the contributions—are allowed to accumulate tax-deferred. As in the case of employer contributions, plan participants pay income taxes on these investment earnings only when they actually receive payments from the plan.

Taxation of Annuity Income

When a contract owner receives payments from an annuity, income taxes then become due. The way in which those earnings are taxed depends upon whether the contract owner is receiving those earnings as annuity payments or as a withdrawal or a surrender from the annuity before the payout period begins.

Taxation of Nonqualified Annuity Payments

When nonqualified annuity payments begin, for purposes of federal income taxes, each payment is considered to consist of two parts:

1. A portion of each payment is considered a return of principal (the amount used to purchase the annuity).

2. The remainder of each payment is considered the contract's earnings.

In the case of a nonqualified annuity, the Internal Revenue Service recognizes that after-tax dollars, which have already been taxed as income, were used to purchase the annuity. Therefore, the contract owner can exclude a portion of each annuity payment from his taxable income by using a formula known as an *exclusion ratio*. The contract owner then pays tax on the portion of the annuity payment that represents investment income but not on the portion that is a return of his tax cost basis.

An exclusion ratio determines what portion of a fixed annuity payment will be exempt from income tax. The exclusion ratio is expressed by the following equation:

$$\text{Exclusion ratio} = \left(\frac{\text{Investment in the contract as of date annuity payments begin}}{\text{Expected return}} \right)$$

Insight 7-1 describes how the exclusion ratio is calculated for one annuitant.

For variable annuity payments, the Internal Revenue Code provides a formula that insurers use to calculate the exclusion amount. The insurer divides the investment in the contract, adjusted for the value of any period certain or refund guarantee, by the number of years over which the annuity will be paid. The monthly *exclusion amount* will remain the same even though the total monthly *payment amount* will fluctuate each month because of the performance of the subaccounts of the variable annuity contract.

With both fixed and variable annuities, the contract owner can only exclude the after-tax dollars paid into the annuity. Once the contract owner has recovered this tax cost basis, he includes the remaining annuity payments in his gross income and they are fully taxable. However, if the annuity starting date was before January 1, 1987, even if the annuitant outlives his life expectancy and recovers his tax cost basis tax-free, the exclusion amount will continue to be applied.

INSIGHT 7.1

The Exclusion Ratio.

Charles LeGrand will begin receiving payments from his fixed annuity on September 1, his 60th birthday. As of September 1, Mr. LeGrand will have paid $50,000 after-tax dollars into his annuity contract. He is scheduled to receive monthly payments of $500 for the remainder of his life.

To determine the exclusion ratio, the amount of his net after-tax contributions is divided by the total return that he expects to receive from the annuity contract. We know from the information above that Mr. LeGrand's investment was $50,000 and that he is scheduled to receive $500 each month

for the rest of his life. (If this amount were to continue for a stated number of months, $500 would be multiplied by that stated number of months.)

IRS Annuity Tables show the life expectancy of an annuitant at a given age. The table below is excerpted from one such table.

Ordinary Life Annuities—One Life—Expected Return Multiples			
Age	Multiple	Age	Multiple
55	28.6	61	23.3
56	27.7	62	22.5
57	26.8	63	21.6
58	25.9	64	20.8
59	25.0	65	20.0
60	24.2	66	19.2

Using this table, an insurer can determine that Mr. LeGrand's life expectancy is 24.2 years, which is 290.4 months. To calculate the total amount Mr. LeGrand is expected to receive, the insurer multiplies his monthly

payment ($500) by the number of months he is expected to live (290.4) to arrive at a total of $145,200. The result of the exclusion ratio is equal to $50,000 (amount invested) divided by $145,200 (amount expected), which

equals 34.4 percent. This means that Mr. LeGrand will receive 34.4 percent ($172) of each $500 annuity payment tax-free; the remainder will be taxable as income. The equation for this calculation is shown below:

$$\left(\frac{\text{Premiums paid}}{\text{Expected return}} \right) = \left(\frac{\$50,000}{(\$500) \times (290.4 \text{ months})} \right) = 34.4\% \text{ excluded}$$

$500 x 34.4% = **$172 each month tax free**

For example, in the case described in Insight 7-1, if Charles LeGrand's annuity starting date falls after January 1, 1987, and if he outlives his life expectancy, then once he recovers his tax cost basis, he includes the remaining annuity payments in his gross income and they are fully taxable. If Mr. LeGrand's annuity starting date falls before January 1, 1987, the exclusion amount would continue to be applied even if he outlived his life expectancy.

Taxation of Qualified Annuity Payments

When an annuity is part of a qualified retirement plan, the plan participant deducts any contributions that he makes from current income. As a result, the money contributed to the annuity has not yet been taxed. Therefore, when the plan participant begins to receive annuity payments, both the principal and the earnings of the qualified annuity will be subject to income taxes. However, if a person has made nondeductible contributions to a 401(k) plan or 403(b) plan, the amount of those contributions would not be taxed.

Taxation of Withdrawals

In Chapter 2, we described the contract provision that allows a nonqualified annuity contract owner to withdraw all or part of the value of the annuity at any time before the annuity payments begin. Withdrawals from annuities are taxed differently than are the annuity payments we just discussed.

Contributions Made After August 13, 1982. Contract owners who made contributions to nonqualified annuity contracts after August 13, 1982, pay taxes according to the *interest first rule*, which states that any amount that the contract owner takes out of the annuity will be considered a withdrawal of the interest (which has not been taxed), until the contract owner has withdrawn all of the interest in the contract. Thereafter, withdrawals are considered to consist of the owner's investment in the contract and are not taxed. Figure 7-4 illustrates how the interest first rule works.

FIGURE 7.4

An Interest First Rule Calculation.

In 1991, Jill Bridges purchased a nonqualified single-premium annuity for $50,000. In 1998, the value of the annuity contract was $75,000. That same year, Ms. Bridges withdrew $10,000 from the contract. The entire amount of the withdrawal was taxable since it was less than the amount of interest earned ($75,000 – $50,000 = $25,000). If she had withdrawn $30,000 from the contract, the first $25,000 would have been treated as interest and would have been taxable income to Ms. Bridges, while the remaining $5,000 would have been treated as a tax-free return of her tax cost basis.

Contributions Made on or Before August 13, 1982. Contributions made to nonqualified annuity contracts on or before August 13, 1982, are taxed using the *cost recovery rule*, which is essentially the opposite of the interest first rule: withdrawals made are considered to be a return of the tax cost basis first and are not considered to be taxable income. After the contract owner withdraws an amount equal to his tax cost basis in the contract, then subsequent withdrawals are considered interest and become taxable to the contract owner as income. Figure 7-5 illustrates how the cost recovery rule works.

FIGURE 7.5

A Cost Recovery Rule Calculation.

Mark Riccio is the contract owner of a $50,000 nonqualified single premium annuity purchased on December 28, 1979. Mr. Riccio withdrew $10,000 from the annuity in 1991. Because the contribution was made before August 13, 1982, Mr. Riccio's $10,000 withdrawal came under the cost recovery rule. The $10,000 was less than the $50,000 Mr. Riccio had invested in the annuity, so his withdrawal was treated as a recovery of the tax cost basis and was not taxable as income.

Penalty Taxes on Withdrawals

To discourage people from purchasing annuities in order to use them as short-term tax-sheltered investments, the federal government has imposed a 10 percent penalty on most *premature distributions*, which are withdrawals of earnings from an annuity made before the contract owner is age 59½. This penalty is in addition to the income taxes that are payable on the amount withdrawn from the annuity and applies to both qualified and nonqualified annuities. The penalty applies only to the taxable portion of the distribution.

Contract owners may be able to avoid the 10 percent penalty tax on premature distribution of earnings in certain circumstances. Some common distributions that are exempt from the premature distribution penalty tax include

◆ Distributions on or after the death of the contract owner (or, if the contract owner is not a natural person, on or after the death of the annuitant)

◆ Distributions that are made while the contract owner is disabled

◆ Distributions that are part of a series of equal periodic payments made for the life of the contract owner or the joint life expectancies of the contract owner and beneficiary

◆ Distributions under an immediate annuity contract

In addition to paying a penalty on a premature distribution, traditional IRA owners and qualified plan participants also pay penalties if they do not begin to receive a *minimum distribution*—a specified amount by a specified age or time—from an account. Qualified retirement plan participants must begin to receive distributions by the later of April 1 of the year after they attain age 70½ or retire. Traditional IRA contract owners must begin receiving a distribution from their accounts no later than April 1 of the year after they attain age 70½. However, contract owners and plan participants who have multiple accounts may choose to receive the total amount required for all of their accounts from one account and not withdraw anything from the others. Owners of Roth IRAs do not have to receive a distribution and may leave their accounts to their heirs tax-free.

Loans and Annuity Contracts

As we mentioned in Chapter 2, contract owners of certain types of annuities are allowed to obtain loans based on the value of their contract. Such loans generally are not a direct withdrawal of money from the annuity contract, but, depending upon the type of annuity, the loan may be considered comparable to a withdrawal and could cause the contract owner to incur a federal income tax obligation and a federal tax penalty for a premature withdrawal.

Loans and Qualified Annuities. Plan participants of certain employer-sponsored qualified annuities—generally 401(k) and 403(b) plans—may obtain a loan from the provider of the annuity contract based on the value of their account balance. The detailed provisions governing such a loan are beyond the scope of this book. For our purposes, the significance of the loan provision in a qualified annuity contract is that the loan is not considered to be a withdrawal in most cases.

For example, a participant in a 401(k) plan is allowed to obtain up to $50,000 or 50 percent of his vested account value, whichever is less, and then make payments with interest to his own account. The plan participant does not pay any federal taxes or tax penalties on the amount of the loan, unless he terminates employment with an unpaid loan balance. In that case, the unpaid portion of the loan is considered to be an early distribution subject to the withholding of 20 percent for federal income taxes and, if the employee is under age 59½, the 10 percent federal tax penalty.

Loans and Nonqualified Annuities. Most nonqualified annuities do not allow loans to be taken directly from the annuity contract balance because this would be considered a distribution. Individual annuity contract owners are prohibited from obtaining loans from IRAs or using their IRAs as security for a bank loan. However, owners of nonqualified annuities may obtain bank loans by using the value of their annuity contract as security, provided the annuity contract has an assignment provision. You'll recall from our discussion in Chapter 2 that an assignment provision grants a nonqualified annuity contract owner the ability to temporarily or permanently transfer ownership of the contract. The tax treatment of a nonqualified annuity used as security for a bank loan differs significantly from a loan that is obtained on a qualified annuity.

Using a nonqualified annuity as security for a bank loan may trigger a taxable event for the contract owner. As we discussed earlier in the chapter, the taxation of the amounts invested in a nonqualified annuity contract before August 13, 1982, and after August 13, 1982, will differ. Therefore, the contract owner may have to pay income tax on the amount of the bank loan that exceeds his investment in the nonqualified annuity contract. In addition, if the contract owner is under age 59½, she may have to pay the 10 percent federal tax penalty for a premature distribution.

For example, suppose that Sara Cullen purchased a nonqualified deferred annuity contract for $50,000 in 1983. In 1998, the surrender value of the annuity contract was $105,000, and Ms. Cullen, who is age 60, used the annuity as collateral to obtain a bank loan in the amount of $75,000. In this situation, the amount of the loan that exceeds Ms. Cullen's investment is $25,000. Therefore, Ms. Cullen must include that $25,000 in her taxable income. However, because Ms. Cullen is older than 59½, she does not have to pay the 10 percent federal tax penalty for a premature distribution.

ESTATE TAXES

One final area of annuity taxation in the United States that we will explore is estate taxes. When a U.S. citizen dies, the federal government imposes estate taxes on the value of a deceased person's estate worth more than $650,000. (This figure is for 1999 and gradually will increase to $1,000,000 by 2006.) These taxes must be paid before the person's property can be distributed to his heirs. One exception to the rule is that a person can transfer all of his estate to a spouse without incurring any estate taxes. A full explanation of estate taxes is beyond the scope of this text; however, we will discuss how estate taxes are calculated on annuity proceeds.

Whether or not an annuity is subject to estate taxation at the contract owner's death depends on whether the contract owner's death falls during the annuity's accumulation period or during the annuity's payout period. If the contract owner dies during the accumulation period, the value of the annuity is included in his *gross estate*, which is the total value of property subject to estate taxes. Whether estate taxes are levied on the deceased's property (including annuity proceeds) depends on the value of the total estate.

If the contract owner dies during the payout period, then two possibilities for estate tax treatment arise, depending on the type of annuity owned. If the annuity was a straight life annuity, then the contract owner's death ends the annuity contract, no more payments are made, and no tax liability is incurred. However, if the contract owner has an annuity that has some type of survivor benefit, then the present value of those future benefits will be included in the contract owner's estate.

SECTION 1035 EXCHANGES

In some instances, a nonqualified annuity contract owner may wish to exchange his annuity for another annuity contract. Because the contract owner technically is withdrawing his premiums and the interest earned from one annuity and using them to purchase another contract, taxation of the deferred income in the original contract becomes an issue. Internal Revenue Code Section 1035 provides for tax-free exchanges of nonqualified annuity contracts within certain guidelines.

Under Section 1035, the following exchanges involving annuities can be made without tax consequences: an annuity can be exchanged for another annuity or a life insurance policy can be exchanged for an annuity. In a Section 1035 exchange, the contract owner transfers the principal and interest from the surrendered contract to the new contract. The same company that issued the original contract might issue the new contract, or a completely different company might issue it. In either case, in order for a Section 1035 exchange to take place, the original insurer must transfer contract values from the original contract to the new contract without any distribution passing through the hands of the contract owner. In addition, the contract owner and annuitant must be the same on the existing contract and the new contract.

ROLLOVERS

When an employee who participates in a qualified retirement plan is no longer employed by the plan's sponsor, he has several options for his vested account balance. If the balance is large enough, he may simply leave it in the account until he retires. However, many people choose a ***rollover***, which is an employee's transfer of retirement funds from one qualified plan to another plan of the same type or to an IRA, without incurring any tax liability. To avoid an automatic withholding of 20 percent for federal income taxes on the rollover, the employee must arrange for a ***trustee transfer*** under which the current plan transfers the money directly to the new plan—or, in the case of an IRA, to the company that has custody of the account. If the employee takes a cash distribution, 20 percent will be withheld for federal income taxes. The employee still can roll over an amount equal to the entire account balance within 60 days of the cash distribution by adding her own money to make up for the 20 percent withheld. She is then eligible to receive a refund of the 20 percent withheld, when she files her federal income tax return.

Canadian Taxation of Annuities

Because the United States offers certain tax advantages to annuities and their contract owners, all of the discussion in this chapter until now has focused on tax treatment of annuities within the United States. In the next section, we will briefly address some aspects of annuity taxation in Canada.

Individual Annuities

Canada taxes the investment income buildup on deferred annuities held by natural persons. This tax is assessed on an annual basis in the case of annuity contracts purchased after 1989 and every three years for contracts purchased before 1989. Corporations and partnerships pay an annual tax on income accumulated in their annuities during the year.

The contract owner includes the full amount of each annuity payment in his taxable income, then deducts the tax cost basis and any portion consisting of amounts previously taxed.

Retirement Plans

Canada's federal *Income Tax Act* encourages private pension plans by according favorable tax treatment to plans registered with Revenue Canada. As in the United States, pension plan participants are not taxed on the amounts in the pension fund until they actually receive pension plan benefits at retirement. Canada currently recognizes the following three forms of retirement plans:

◆ Registered pension plans

◆ Deferred profit sharing plans

◆ Registered retirement savings plans

As we noted in Chapter 6, registered pension plans (RPPs) are the Canadian equivalent of the qualified retirement plans available in the United States. Contributions to RPPs by plan participants and employers are tax deductible, and are subject to specified annual maximum amounts. Most of these plans require participants to contribute. Usually, the plan sponsor's contribution is a specified percentage of the participant's contribution.

In a *deferred profit sharing plan (DPSP)*, plan sponsor contributions are related to profits and are tax deductible by the plan sponsor, subject to specified annual maximum amounts much like the profit sharing plans available in the United States. Participant contributions cannot be required and are not tax deductible. In fact, after 1991, participant contributions are no longer permitted.

Much like individual retirement arrangements (IRAs) available in the United States, *registered retirement savings plans (RRSPs)* allow people with earned income (not employers) to make tax-deductible contributions, subject to specified annual maximum amounts, into a tax-deferred savings plan. Some employers have established group RRSPs—which are basically a collection of individual RRSPs, but which offer employees the advantage of making contributions through payroll deductions. Employers may make contributions to group RRSPs on behalf of their employees. However, participants report employer contributions as wages and then take an offsetting deduction in the amount of the contribution. Thus, any employer contributions become employee contributions for tax purposes.

KEY TERMS AND CONCEPTS

income tax
before-tax dollars
after-tax dollars
tax cost basis
exclusion ratio
interest first rule
cost recovery rule
premature distributions
minimum distribution
gross estate
rollover
trustee transfer
deferred profit sharing plan (DPSP)
registered retirement savings plans (RRSPs)

CHAPTER 8

Regulation of the Annuity Industry

After studying this chapter, you should be able to

◆ Describe the role and function of the National Association of Insurance Commissioners (NAIC)

◆ Explain the purpose of solvency regulation

◆ Discuss the various aspects of market conduct regulation—licensing, contract forms and provisions, advertising, and disclosure

◆ Explain the purpose of market conduct regulation

◆ Explain the major focus of federal regulation of the annuity industry in the United States

◆ Discuss the functions of the Securities and Exchange Commission (SEC) and the National Association of Securities Dealers (NASD) as they relate to the annuity industry

◆ Discuss annuity regulations at the provincial and federal levels in Canada

Because thousands of people own annuities and rely on them for future financial security, the sale and issue of annuity products is subject to extensive regulation. Both the United States and Canada have developed regulatory systems to ensure that insurance companies and the people and agencies that sell annuity products conduct their business fairly and ethically and can meet their financial obligations. In this chapter, we will look at the various government agencies that regulate annuity products and the companies and people who sell them. Our discussion will focus primarily on annuity regulation in the United States; however, we will also consider comparable regulation of annuities in Canada.

STATE REGULATION

In the United States, the state governments—not the federal government—have primary authority to regulate the insurance industry. In 1945, the U.S. Congress enacted the *McCarran-Ferguson Act*, under which it agreed to leave insurance regulation to the states as long as it considered state regulation to be adequate. The regulatory authority granted to the states by the Act extends to the sale and issue of annuity products.

However, Congress maintains the right to enact insurance legislation if it determines that state regulation is inadequate or not in the public interest.

In order to protect consumers, the states have enacted a variety of laws to regulate the insurance companies that do business within their borders. The states also regulate the various products that each insurer sells. To manage this regulatory function, each state has established an administrative agency, typically known as the *state insurance department*, which is charged with assuring that insurance companies operating within the state comply with all of that state's insurance laws and regulations. Usually, each state insurance department is under the direction of a state insurance commissioner or state superintendent of insurance.

In most respects, the insurance laws of the various states are similar because they are based on model laws and regulations developed by the *National Association of Insurance Commissioners (NAIC)*, which is a private, nonprofit organization consisting of the insurance commissioners or superintendents of the various state insurance departments. The NAIC promotes uniformity of state regulation by developing model laws and regulations that each state is encouraged to pass. A *model law* is sample legislation developed by the NAIC that state legislatures can adopt into law exactly as written or use as a basis for developing their own legislation. State legislatures also can develop their own laws without using NAIC model laws as a guide.

Because annuities are considered insurance products, many state insurance regulations that apply to insurance policies also apply to annuities. However, many states have passed additional laws to regulate the sale and issue of annuities. Figure 8-1 summarizes several NAIC model laws that form the basis for much of this legislation.

Whether based on NAIC model laws or developed independently, state regulations governing insurance companies and insurance products generally fall into two broad categories.

1. *Solvency regulation.* **Solvency** is the ability of an insurer to make specified payments to contract owners and to meet other financial obligations on time. Solvency regulations address the need for insurance companies to be financially stable and capable of paying debts and disbursing life insurance benefits and annuity proceeds—such as death benefits or annuity payments—when they are due.

2. *Market conduct regulation.* **Market conduct** is the manner in which an insurer carries out its various business activities. Market conduct regulation addresses the need for insurance companies to conduct business fairly and ethically. Among other things, market conduct regulations govern licensing procedures, content of contract forms, required contract provisions, product advertising standards, and disclosure requirements.

Using these two categories, let's take a closer look at the major state regulations that govern the sale and issue of annuities.

Solvency Regulation

The financial stability of an insurance company is an important concern for people who own insurance and annuity products. For this reason, each state has enacted laws that require any insurance company operating within the state to demonstrate that it can pay benefits to contract owners and meet its other financial obligations. State regulators monitor the financial condition of an insurer by reviewing the company's **Annual Statement**, which is a financial report containing detailed accounting and statistical data about the company. The states require each insurer doing business in the state to prepare an Annual Statement every year and file it with the state insurance department. Each insurer is also required to file its Annual Statement with the NAIC. In addition, regulators perform a detailed examination of each insurer's operations and financial condition at least every three to five years—more often if they believe doing so is necessary.

FIGURE 8.1

NAIC Model Laws Pertaining to the Sale and Issue of Annuities.

Standard Nonforfeiture Law for Individual Deferred Annuities

Requires that individual deferred annuity contracts contain certain nonforfeiture provisions, such as
- Provisions providing options for continuing the annuity in the event premium payments are stopped
- A provision allowing deferral of payment of the cash surrender value by the insurer
- A provision that requires disclosure of information on interest rates, surrender and death benefits, and mortality tables used in any calculations to be included in the annuity contract

Model Variable Annuity Regulation

Establishes special guidelines that govern variable annuity contracts
- Regulates the use of separate accounts for annuity investments and the use of benefit illustrations
- Mandates the inclusion of disclosure provisions, grace period provisions, reinstatement provisions, and nonforfeiture benefits provisions
- Requires that investment reports be distributed to contract owners
- Establishes agent qualifications required to sell variable annuities

New Annuity Mortality Table Model Rule

Recognizes certain new mortality tables as the minimum standard of valuation for annuity contracts

Replacement of Life Insurance and Annuities Model Regulation

Specifies the procedures an insurer must follow when issuing a new contract that will replace an existing contract
- Requires both the insurer and the applicant to sign a statement indicating that the contract applied for will replace an existing contract
- Requires the insurer to provide the applicant with a written document entitled "Notice Regarding Replacement"
- Requires the replacing insurer to notify the insurer that issued the existing contract that the contract may be replaced

Rules Governing the Advertising of Life Insurance (and Annuities)

Establishes minimum standards that require insurers to disclose to the public all relevant information in their advertisements for life insurance and annuity products

Model Annuity and Deposit Fund Disclosure Regulation

Establishes disclosure requirements for individual deferred annuities and certain group annuities
- Requires that prospective annuity buyers be provided with basic information about annuities, and information regarding premiums, cash values, and surrender costs for the specific annuity contract the prospective buyer is considering

(Note: At the time of this writing, the NAIC is developing a new model regulation that will address annuity disclosure and illustration requirements.)

In the event an insurer is unable to meet its financial obligations, state law protects the insurer's customers against loss—up to a specified sum. Each state has formed a ***guaranty association***, which is an agency that is composed of all the life insurance companies operating in the state and that is established to cover the financial obligations of member companies that go out of business. Typically, a guaranty association provides funds to guarantee payment for certain policies, including annuities, up to certain limits. To fund payment of these obligations, the guaranty association in each state imposes mandatory assessments on all association member companies in the state. Each insurer's share of the total assessment is set according to the insurer's share of the total premiums written in that state; however, each state limits the maximum amount that an insurer is required to contribute in a given year.

Market Conduct Regulation

In addition to the solvency examinations we mentioned in the previous section, insurance regulators also formally monitor market conduct to verify that insurers and their sales personnel are adhering to regulatory standards governing market activity.

Market conduct regulations govern a variety of insurance company activities in the areas of both sales and administrative operations. In regard to annuities, we will consider three general categories of regulations that fall within the realm of market conduct: (1) licensing, (2) contract forms and contract provisions, and (3) advertising and disclosure.

State Licensing

The laws and regulations of the state in which an insurance company is incorporated govern the operations of that insurance company. Before an insurance company begins conducting business and selling insurance and annuity products within a given state, the company must obtain a license from the state's insurance department. An insurance company must be licensed by each state in which it conducts business.

Generally, insurers are required to obtain a license for insurance and annuity sales in each state in which they

- ◆ Solicit applications for insurance products, including annuities
- ◆ Issue and deliver insurance and annuity contracts
- ◆ Collect premiums for insurance and annuity contracts
- ◆ Maintain an office that transacts insurance business

An insurer must satisfy a variety of state-mandated requirements in order to obtain a license. Most licensing requirements are intended to ensure that only reputable and financially stable companies are selling insurance and annuity products in the state. We will not discuss these requirements in detail; however, we should note that annuities are generally treated, for regulatory purposes, as if they were a type of life insurance. Therefore, in most states, an insurer that is licensed to sell life insurance is also licensed to sell annuities. Most states, however, require insurers to obtain specific authority to sell variable life insurance and variable annuity products.

In addition to state regulations governing licensing procedures for insurance companies, the states have developed legislation establishing specific requirements that insurance sales representatives must satisfy in order to sell insurance and annuity products. These requirements are similar in nature to the requirements imposed upon insurance companies and they help ensure that sales representatives are reputable and knowledgeable about the products they sell.

Generally, in order to sell annuity products in a given state, a person must first be licensed to sell life insurance in that state. Some states require a separate license to sell annuities. Sales representatives typically must renew their licenses every year and may need to periodically participate in continuing education courses as a condition of license renewal. In addition, a state may revoke a sales representative's license if she engages in illegal or unethical practices.

Contract Forms and Contract Provisions

Each state also regulates the contract forms that insurers may use within the state. An insurance company, therefore, must file with the insurance department each contract form it plans to use. The insurance department reviews the form to make certain it contains all required provisions and is not unfair or deceptive in any way. Many states have also passed laws, known as **readability requirements**, that require insurers to reduce the amount of technical jargon and legal language included in insurance and annuity contracts. The purpose of these requirements is to help ensure that consumers understand the terms of the contract they are purchasing. A contract form that does not meet a state's readability requirements will not be approved for use in that state.

In addition, state insurance laws generally require that all individual annuity contracts include certain provisions. These provisions are designed to ensure that annuity contract owners are treated fairly. Figure 8-2 summarizes these provisions, most of which we discussed in detail in Chapter 2.

In addition to these contract provisions, state regulations generally require an applicant for an annuity to indicate whether the coverage applied for will replace any existing coverage. Most states have adopted legislation—based on the NAIC Replacement of Life Insurance and Annuities Model Regulation—that specifies the procedures an insurer must follow when an applicant responds with a "yes" to the replacement question. The issuer of the replacement annuity must notify the issuer of the original contract that the applicant intends to cancel that contract and replace it with a new contract. In addition, the insurer must ensure that the annuity applied for is a suitable replacement for the existing contract, especially when dealing with variable annuity contracts. We will consider suitability requirements for variable annuities in greater detail later in this chapter.

FIGURE 8.2

Required Individual Annuity Contract Provisions.

Provision	Description
Entire contract provision	Specifies that only those documents attached to or appearing in the annuity contract are part of the contract
Free-look provision	Gives the contract owner a specified period within which to return the annuity contract and receive a refund of all premiums paid
Misstatement of age or sex provision	Provides for the adjustment of benefits if the annuitant's age or sex was misstated in the application
Incontestability provision	States that the insurer, in most instances, cannot contest the validity of the annuity contract after it becomes effective
Dividend provision	For participating annuities, describes the contract owner's right to receive dividends and the dividend payment options available
Nonforfeiture provision	For individual deferred annuities, states the benefit amounts that the insurer will pay if premium payments stop or the contract is surrendered
Payout options provision	Describes the contract owner's right to receive benefits and the payout options available

Advertising and Disclosure Requirements

In addition to requirements regarding licenses, contract forms, and contract provisions, most states impose certain standards regarding annuity advertising by the companies and people who sell annuity products. Many state requirements regarding annuity advertising are based on the NAIC Rules Governing the Advertising of Life Insurance. State legislation based on the NAIC Rules is intended to ensure fair and honest representation of annuity products during the sales process.

For annuity regulatory purposes, any materials used in the sale of an annuity product are considered advertisements. These materials include

◆ Promotional materials, including direct mail, radio, television, and print advertisements

◆ Sales aids, including brochures, pamphlets, letters, and sales illustrations

◆ Materials used to recruit or train sales representatives

◆ Prepared sales talks, presentations, and other materials used by sales representatives in the sales process

Insurers must adhere to specific guidelines when preparing material for use in the sales process. All materials must clearly identify the product being sold and the name of the insurer issuing the contract. Further, no material may contain any false or misleading information or include unfair or incomplete comparisons to the products of other insurers.

Some states have also developed detailed annuity disclosure standards—based on the NAIC Model Annuity and Deposit Fund Disclosure Regulation—that require insurers to provide prospective buyers of specific types of annuities with information to help them select an annuity appropriate to their needs. Under these regulations, insurers must provide prospective buyers of certain types of annuities with a ***Buyer's Guide to Annuities***, which is a publication that describes the various types of annuities available and some of the annuity features that consumers should consider before purchasing an annuity. In addition, the insurer must provide a ***contract summary***, which is a document that contains relevant contract and benefit information for the specific annuity that a consumer is considering purchasing.

At the time of this writing, the NAIC is developing a new model regulation that (1) would impose additional disclosure requirements on insurers that sell annuities and (2) would impose requirements on the use of annuity sales illustrations.

FEDERAL REGULATION

Although most insurance company regulation in the United States is conducted by the states, some insurance and annuity products are subject to federal laws. The insurance and annuity products that are subject to federal regulation are those that have an investment component that requires the contract owner to assume some or all of the risk associated with securities held in a separate account. As we noted in Chapter 4, the securities industry in the United States is regulated by the Securities and Exchange Commission (SEC). The SEC has determined that some insurance products, such as variable annuities, are investment products as well as insurance products, and, as such, must be registered as securities with the SEC. Insurers that issue these variable insurance products must comply with federal laws that govern securities, in addition to complying with state insurance laws. Many of the regulations pertaining to these products are contained in the following four pieces of federal legislation:

- ◆ The Securities Act of 1933
- ◆ The Securities Exchange Act of 1934
- ◆ The Investment Company Act of 1940
- ◆ The Investment Advisers Act of 1940

The ***Securities Act of 1933*** protects investors by requiring that they receive specified types of information about securities being offered for sale to the public. The Act also prohibits misrepresentation and fraud in the sale of securities. To enforce the Securities Act of 1933, the U.S. Congress passed the *Securities Exchange Act of 1934*, which created the SEC and granted it broad authority to regulate the securities industry.

The *Investment Company Act of 1940* regulates the conduct of investment companies. An *investment company* is a company that issues securities and engages primarily in investing and trading securities. The Act requires all investment companies to register with the SEC. Although the SEC does not consider an insurance company that is primarily engaged in the business of insurance to be an investment company, the SEC does consider an insurance company's separate account to be an investment company, which must be registered with the SEC.

The Investment Company Act of 1940 further requires a registered investment company to disclose specific information about its financial condition and investment policies so that investors have accurate and complete information about the company. Investment companies must comply with the Act by registering all of the securities they issue—including variable annuities—with the SEC.

Finally, the *Investment Advisers Act of 1940* regulates the conduct of investment advisers. An *investment adviser* is a firm or person who is compensated in exchange for providing advice to investors about the value of securities and the potential advantages and disadvantages of buying and selling securities. Any firm or person providing such services must register with the SEC and must conduct business in accordance with SEC regulations.

National Association of Securities Dealers

In addition to registering with the SEC, investment companies and investment advisers must also register with the *National Association of Securities Dealers (NASD)*, which is a nonprofit organization of securities dealers responsible for regulating the market conduct of member companies and representatives.

The NASD was established by the SEC in 1938. The NASD establishes licensing standards and codes of conduct for investment companies, investment advisers, sales representatives, sales support personnel, and customer service personnel at member companies. Investment advisers and sales representatives who want to market securities products—including variable annuities—must register with the NASD, disclose certain background information to the NASD, and take special examinations offered by the NASD. As we mentioned earlier, sales representatives who sell annuities—including variable annuities—must also be licensed as insurance agents at the state level.

The NASD also requires certain people in sales support and customer service positions to register with the NASD. Generally, NASD registration is required for personnel who facilitate the deposit, transfer, or withdrawal of funds from a variable annuity or other federally regulated securities product.

Sales representatives and other personnel who have registered with the NASD, disclosed the required background information, and passed one or more NASD examinations are known as ***registered representatives.*** Figure 8-3 summarizes the types of registration categories most commonly required for variable annuity sales representatives, sales support staff, and customer service personnel.

FIGURE 8.3

NASD Registration Categories.

	Title	Description
Series 6	Investment Company/ Variable Contract Representative	Required to sell mutual funds and variable annuities. May be required for sales support and customer service staff.
Series 26	Investment Company/ Variable Contract Principal	Required to supervise registered representatives selling mutual funds and variable annuities.
Series 7	General Securities Representative	Required to sell bonds and stocks. Can be used in place of Series 6 to sell mutual funds and variable annuities. May be required for sales support and customer service staff.
Series 24	General Securities Principal	Required to supervise registered representatives selling bonds and stocks. Can be used in place of Series 26 to supervise registered representatives selling mutual funds and annuities.
Series 63	Uniform Securities Representative	Required to sell securities products; emphasis on regulations and compliance.

Registration

Both the SEC and the NASD closely monitor the activities of member companies and registered representatives. Three areas that these agencies closely monitor are

- ◆ Suitability
- ◆ Disclosure
- ◆ Advertising

Suitability

As we mentioned earlier in this chapter, state regulations require insurers to establish that a customer is making a suitable purchase whenever any newly issued annuity contract is replacing an existing annuity. NASD rules require an insurer to follow a similar procedure when issuing new variable annuity contracts. Registered representatives who sell variable annuities must have reasonable grounds for believing each recommendation they make to a customer—including each recommendation regarding variable annuity products—is suitable based on the customer's financial situation and objectives. Thus, before making any product recommendations, a representative must obtain a basic understanding of the customer's current and future financial needs. When a customer applies for a new variable annuity contract, the registered representative must complete a suitability statement at the time of the annuity sale. Information included in the suitability statement is intended to enable the registered representative to provide sound and informed financial advice to the buyer regarding the variable annuity. Buyers do not have to provide the information requested, but must sign a waiver if they refuse to do so. Insight 8-1 discusses some of the suitability issues a registered representative faces when recommending a variable annuity product to a customer.

INSIGHT 8.1

Enforcement Spotlight: Variable Products.

Variable products are issued by insurance companies and are considered insurance contracts subject to regulation under state law. Variable contracts are also securities because owners assume investment risks. The result is that variable products are regulated by the NASD and SEC because they are securities, and by the state insurance regulators because they are insurance products.

Variable products are subject to the same suitability requirements as any other security. In recommending the purchase, sale, or exchange of any security, a registered representative must have reasonable grounds for believing that the recommendation is suitable based upon the customer's financial objectives and needs.

Some factors should be considered when recommending the purchase of a variable product.

◆ Are the life insurance needs of the customer already adequately met?

◆ Does the customer express a desire for financial protection afforded by an instrument other than an insurance product?

◆ Does the customer fully appreciate how much of the purchase payment or premium is allocated to cover insurance or other costs?

◆ Does the customer understand the complexity of variable products?

◆ What are the customer's investment objectives?

◆ Is the customer willing to invest a set amount on a yearly basis?

◆ What is the customer's tolerance for risk?

◆ What are the customer's needs for liquidity and short-term investments?

◆ What are the customer's needs for retirement income?

◆ What is the customer's investment sophistication, including the ability to monitor the performance of the separate account?

Source: Adapted from David L. Snyder, "Enforcement Spotlight: Variable Products," *LIMRA's MarketFacts* (September/October 1998): 10. Used with permission.

Disclosure

In addition to establishing the suitability of the annuity contract for the applicant, federal regulations require that the insurer provide each prospective variable annuity buyer with a ***prospectus***, which is a written document describing specific aspects of the security being offered for sale. The prospectus must contain information explaining the investment philosophy and objectives of the separate account, any fund expenses and fees, and past performance of subaccounts within the separate account. Neither the prospectus nor any contract illustration used in the sales process can project future subaccount values based on past investment experience. However, the use of hypothetical assumed rates of return to illustrate possible subaccount values is allowed.

In addition, the SEC requires insurers to provide the owners of variable annuity contracts with an annual report of separate account activity. The report must detail (1) fund expenses and fees for the period covered, (2) investment performance and account values for all subaccounts in which the contract owner has funds invested, and (3) any changes in a subaccount's investment strategy or major holdings.

Advertising

The SEC and NASD impose strict requirements on advertisements and sales materials used to promote securities products, including variable annuities. These requirements are similar in most aspects to the state regulations governing annuity advertisements and sales materials that we discussed earlier. However, some additional standards apply to variable annuities.

- ◆ Materials must contain the name of the registered representative who is selling the annuity.

- ◆ Materials must not contain any promises of specific investment results, including predictions and projections.

- ◆ Materials must not imply that any state or federal regulatory body has endorsed or approved the product or the registered representative selling the product.

EQUITY-INDEXED ANNUITIES AND MARKET VALUE ADJUSTED ANNUITIES

As we have mentioned, depending on the specific features of the product, an equity-indexed or market value adjusted annuity may be subject to federal regulation as a security. At the time of this writing, most equity-indexed and market value adjusted annuities are not registered with the SEC.

An annuity or other life insurance product must meet a three-part test in order to be exempt from federal securities registration with the SEC.

1. The contract must be issued by a corporation subject to the supervision of a state insurance commissioner, bank commissioner, or similar state regulator.

2. The contract's investment risk must be borne primarily by the issuer of the contract.

3. The product must not be marketed primarily as an investment.

Equity-indexed annuities and market value adjusted annuities generally satisfy these requirements, because they are issued by insurers and are therefore subject to the supervision of a state insurance commissioner. Further, funds used to purchase these types of annuities usually are placed in an insurer's general account, and the insurer assumes most of the investment risk for these funds. However, despite minimum interest rate guarantees, equity-indexed annuities generally guarantee the return of only 90 percent of the initial investment. The owners of market value adjusted annuities, too, may lose a portion of their initial investment. The SEC has expressed concern because, in addition to the risk of loss, the nature of these products makes marketing them without emphasizing their investment aspects particularly difficult. For these reasons, the SEC is currently reviewing these products to determine whether they are primarily insurance products exempt from federal regulation or whether they are primarily investments and therefore subject to federal securities regulation.

CANADIAN REGULATION

Regulations governing the insurance and annuity industry in Canada are similar to regulations in the United States. In Canada, the federal and provincial governments share the responsibility for developing and enforcing legislation to regulate insurance and annuity sales and insurance company operations. In Canada, an insurance company may be incorporated under the authority of either the federal government or one of the provincial governments. Both levels of government maintain authority to regulate the financial soundness of insurance companies. However, each provincial government regulates how insurers conduct business within the province.

Provincial Legislation

Each province or territory has enacted laws to regulate insurance within the province or territory. In most respects, these laws are similar throughout Canada, but some differences do exist, especially between the laws of Quebec and the laws of other provinces and territories.

Each province has established an administrative agency to enforce the province's insurance laws and regulations. Typically, this agency is known as the *Office of the Superintendent of Insurance* and operates under the direction of an individual known as the *Superintendent of Insurance*. The various provincial superintendents of insurance have voluntarily formed a collective body known as the *Canadian Council of Insurance Regulators (CCIR)*. Much like their counterparts on the NAIC in the United States, CCIR members discuss insurance issues and recommend uniform insurance legislation to the provinces. Provincial regulation of life insurance and annuity contracts is fairly uniform because most provinces have enacted laws based on model legislation recommended by the CCIR.

As with state regulations in the United States, provincial regulations focus on two main areas of insurance company sales and operations—solvency and market conduct.

Solvency Regulation

Each province has developed solvency regulation to monitor the financial stability of insurers. Solvency laws require each province's Office of the

Superintendent of Insurance to supervise companies that were incorporated by the province and to examine those companies periodically to ensure they are able to meet their financial obligations—such as making benefit payments to an annuitant or annuity contract beneficiary—as they come due.

To avoid duplication of solvency regulation, the provinces generally have agreed that provincially incorporated companies will be supervised by the province in which the insurer was incorporated. The provinces rely on the federal government to supervise federally registered companies. Each province, however, retains the right to supervise the operations of any insurer that operates within that province.

Market Conduct Regulation

Each province in Canada regulates the operations of insurance companies within its borders in order to protect contract owners. Provincial laws also address the need for insurance companies to conduct business fairly and ethically.

In order to operate within a province, an insurance company must first obtain a license from the province.

In addition, each person who plans to sell life insurance and annuity products must obtain the appropriate sales license from the province. Licensing requirements and standards of conduct for sales representatives in Canada are similar to those governing U.S. sales representatives.

Provincial laws also govern the contract forms that are used within each province. However, the provinces do not require that all contract forms be filed before they are issued. Insurers are required to file contract forms in only the following two situations: (1) as a condition of obtaining a license to conduct an insurance business within the province and (2) before marketing a variable life insurance contract in the province. However, most insurers regularly file all their contract forms with the provincial superintendent of insurance. In addition, provincial regulations require the inclusion of certain provisions in all annuity contracts. These are similar to the provisions required by state regulators in the United States.

Federal Regulation in Canada

The **Insurance Companies Act** is the primary federal law that governs insurance companies operating in Canada. The Act includes a number of provisions that address the need for insurance companies to be financially stable and capable of paying debts and disbursing life insurance benefits and annuity proceeds—such as death benefits or annuity payments—when they come due. The Act applies to all (1) federally incorporated insurers, (2) foreign insurers, and (3) provincially incorporated insurers that conduct business outside their province of incorporation. Recall that insurance companies can incorporate through either the federal or provincial governments in Canada. Most insurers opt for federal incorporation.

A federal agency, the ***Office of the Superintendent of Financial Institutions (OSFI)***, under the direction of the Superintendent of Financial Institutions, is responsible for monitoring the operations of all financial institutions in Canada, including life insurance companies. The Inspector General of Financial Institutions monitors the operations of insurance companies incorporated in Quebec.

Every insurance company that is subject to federal regulation must prepare an Annual Return each year and file it with the appropriate regulatory agency. The ***Annual Return*** is a financial report that contains detailed accounting and statistical data about the insurer—similar to the data provided on the Annual Statement filed by insurers in the United States. The Insurance Companies Act requires OSFI to periodically examine the financial condition of each federally regulated insurer; an examination is required at least every three years but can be conducted more often if the superintendent believes an earlier examination is necessary.

KEY TERMS AND CONCEPTS

McCarran-Ferguson Act
state insurance department
National Association of Insurance Commissioners (NAIC)
model law
solvency
market conduct
Annual Statement
guaranty association
readability requirements
Buyer's Guide to Annuities
contract summary
Securities Act of 1933
Securities Exchange Act of 1934
Investment Company Act of 1940
investment company
Investment Advisers Act of 1940
investment adviser
National Association of Securities Dealers (NASD)
registered representative
prospectus
Office of the Superintendent of Insurance
Canadian Council of Insurance Regulators (CCIR)
Insurance Companies Act
Office of the Superintendent of Financial Institutions (OSFI)
Annual Return

CHAPTER 9

Marketing and Distributing Annuities

After studying this chapter, you should be able to

◆ Define *markets* and *marketing* and list the components of the marketing mix

◆ List and discuss the stages in the product development process

◆ Describe several ways an insurer can promote its annuity products

◆ Explain what a distribution system is and discuss the types of personal selling distribution systems and direct response distribution systems that insurers use to sell annuity products

In the preceding chapters, we discussed the various types of annuities sold by insurers and the typical provisions contained in these products. We also looked at the regulatory and tax environment within which annuities are sold in the United States and Canada. In this chapter, we will examine how insurers sell annuities. We will begin our discussion with an overview of marketing terms and concepts. We will then discuss the process of product development. Finally, we will explain how insurance companies promote and distribute annuity products.

MARKETING BASICS

Marketing is the process of planning and executing product development, pricing, promotion, and distribution in order to create exchanges that satisfy the needs and objectives of both buyers and sellers. An *exchange* occurs whenever one party—a buyer—gives something of value to another party—a seller—in order to receive something of value in return. In the context of annuity marketing, a contract owner exchanges money, in the form of a premium, in return for an annuity contract in which the insurer promises to provide certain benefits to the contract owner.

The four elements included in our definition of marketing—product, price, promotion, and distribution—are the major factors that a company considers when determining how best to meet consumer needs. These elements are collectively known as the *marketing mix*. In the context of the marketing mix, *product* refers to a good, service, or idea that a seller offers to buyers in order to satisfy their needs. *Price* refers to an item of value that a buyer gives to a seller in exchange for a product; typically, price refers to an amount of money. *Promotion* refers to the activities that sellers use to communicate with buyers in order to influence them to purchase a product. *Distribution* refers to the activities that sellers engage in to make products available for consumers to buy. Later in this chapter, we will discuss the marketing mix as it relates to the marketing of annuities. We will focus on product development, promotion, and distribution. Product pricing for annuities is a complex topic beyond the scope of this text.

In order to successfully develop, price, promote, and distribute new products and services, insurance companies must conduct extensive market research in order to determine where their customers are located and what types of products and services they need. In this context, a **market** is a group of people who, either as individuals or as members of organizations, are the actual or potential buyers of a product. Insurers typically use market research data as a means to identify specific **market segments**, which are groups of consumers who share common needs or characteristics. The process of dividing the total market for a product into groups of consumers who share common needs or characteristics is known as **market segmentation**. To define market segments, insurers generally look at such factors as age, gender, income, education, spending patterns, occupation, and geographic location.

Generally, a company's marketing efforts are more effective when they are focused on smaller groups of consumers with similar needs rather than on larger groups of consumers whose needs are not as closely aligned. For this reason, many insurers engage in **target marketing**, which is the process of evaluating various market segments and then selecting one or more market segment—called a **target market**—on which to focus the company's marketing efforts. Knowing the general characteristics and needs of a target market helps the insurer to develop and distribute products and services that will be attractive to the consumers in that market.

For example, consider an insurer whose target market consists of middle-income retirees who have a need to supplement their retirement income. Typically, market research will reveal that these consumers are interested in financial products that guarantee the safety of investment principal and provide a regular monthly income. Knowing these facts, an insurer might decide to develop a fixed annuity product to sell in this target market.

Now consider an insurer whose target market consists of upper-income persons in their mid-40s who have a need to accumulate money for retirement. Generally, market research will reveal that consumers in this group are willing to accept some risk and are interested in financial products that can offer the potential for long-term growth. Knowing these facts, an insurer might decide to develop a variable annuity product to sell in this target market.

Finally, to coordinate all the marketing efforts of the company, insurers typically develop a **marketing plan**, which is a plan that specifies the company's overall marketing objectives, the strategies needed to achieve those objectives, and the specific sales goals for each product or line of products the company offers.

PRODUCT DEVELOPMENT

If an insurer didn't have a product to sell, it wouldn't have anything to market. Therefore, the marketing process for an insurer usually begins with product development. In this context, product development includes developing new products that have never before been offered by the company, adding new products to an existing product line, and modifying products currently offered in order to increase their appeal to consumers.

The process of developing new, or enhancing existing, annuity products typically requires the expertise of staff from many functional areas within an insurance company. Personnel from a company's marketing, sales, actuarial, investment, information systems, customer service, legal, and accounting departments must all work together to ensure that new annuity products or product enhancements (1) satisfy consumer needs, (2) meet company objectives, (3) comply with applicable state and federal regulations, and (4) can be supported by the company's human, financial, and technological resources.

Although the precise details of the product development process differ from company to company, the process generally consists of a common set of research, planning, design, and product review activities. Figure 9-1 presents an overview of the typical stages in the product development process.

FIGURE 9.1

Stages in the Product Development Process.

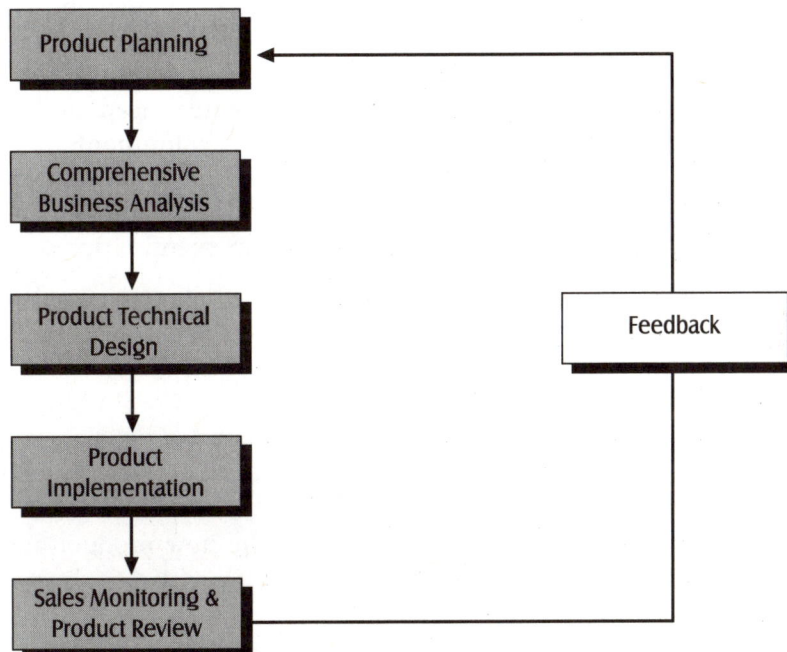

Product Planning

For any insurer, the product development process begins with an idea. It could be an idea for a new product or line of products, or for the redesign of an existing product or group of products. The idea may come from a special committee established by an insurer to generate new product ideas or it may come from a home office employee, a field sales representative, a consumer group, or from some other source—either inside or outside the company.

Many insurance companies establish product development teams composed of staff from various departments who meet on a regular basis to review the insurer's overall product development strategy and to develop and evaluate ideas for new or enhanced products. At this stage in the product planning process, the product development team typically considers, but does not closely scrutinize, all ideas that are consistent with the overall objectives of the company and the needs of its target markets.

Not all product ideas can be acted upon at the same time. Typically, after a number of product ideas are generated, the ideas undergo a screening process to determine which ones merit further investigation and development. During the **screening process** the product development team quickly scrutinizes product ideas and weeds out those ideas that are not consistent with the insurer's current or future marketing plans.

Comprehensive Business Analysis

After screening product ideas, the product development team performs a **comprehensive business analysis**, which is a preliminary review of market conditions and other factors designed to determine the feasibility of any product ideas that appear to meet consumer needs and company objectives. During this phase of the product development process, the insurer's marketing department typically conducts a **market analysis**, which is a study of all the environmental factors that might affect sales of the product. A typical market analysis includes an examination of

- ◆ Target markets
- ◆ Consumers' needs
- ◆ Competitors' activities
- ◆ Distribution systems
- ◆ Field sales force requirements
- ◆ The relationship between the new product and the products the company currently offers

In addition, during this stage, the product development team compiles a list of **product design objectives** that specify a product's basic characteristics, features, benefits, and the manner in which the benefits will be provided. For an annuity, these design objectives could include basic product characteristics such as contract charges and fees, interest guarantees and interest crediting frequency, investment options, surrender provisions, death benefits, and annuity payout provisions. The product development team also prepares a marketing plan for the product. Then, the product development team estimates preliminary pricing, sales, revenue, cost, and profit figures.

Finally, the product development team prepares a product proposal containing all of the data gathered during the comprehensive business analysis. Executives at the company evaluate the proposal and determine whether to accept it, reject it, or send it back to the product development team for further analysis.

Product Technical Design

After the executives at an insurance company approve a product proposal, the product moves on to the technical design stage. During this stage, the product design objectives specified in the product proposal are reviewed and refined. Because of the varied and complex tasks involved in designing a new annuity product or enhancement, virtually every functional area of an insurance company can become involved at this stage. Figure 9-2 lists some of the typical activities performed during the technical design stage for a new product or product enhancement.

FIGURE 9.2

Typical Activities Performed During Product Technical Design.

Marketing and sales personnel review the product to determine its potential appeal to consumers and the ease with which the company can promote, distribute, and sell the product.

Actuaries scrutinize the product's rate structure and other product features to assure it is financially sound.

Representatives from the investment area determine what types of investments are necessary to make the product successful.

The accounting department determines what, if any, special accounting procedures must be developed to manage accounts for the product.

The company's lawyers or compliance department staff review product specifications to assure compliance with all applicable state and federal regulations.

Customer service and administrative staff determine what procedures are needed to support the product.

Staff from the information systems department are asked to identify the type of computer systems the company will need to administer the product.

By the end of the technical design stage, the product's features, provisions, and pricing structure are finalized, and contract forms are created.

Product Implementation

Following the technical design stage, the product moves on to the implementation stage. At this stage in the product development process, the company files contract forms with the appropriate state, provincial, and federal regulatory agencies in order to obtain legal permission to market the product. The marketing department develops detailed plans to promote the product and designs training materials for the company's sales and administrative personnel. Employees throughout the company begin to put into place the people, procedures, and technology needed to support the product.

After an insurer has received approval to market a product and it has put into place the systems needed to support the product, the insurer is ready to introduce the product to consumers. Product introduction is the culmination of all the product development activities we have discussed thus far. At this time the insurer begins to promote and actively distribute the product to consumers in its target markets. However, the product development process does not end when a product is introduced.

Sales Monitoring and Product Review

After a new product has been introduced to an insurer's target markets, the product development process continues with sales monitoring and product review. This stage in the product development process helps an insurer determine whether a product meets both the needs of the insurer's target markets and the sales goals the insurer has established. Because most insurers use sales and marketing data to generate ideas for new products or product enhancements, information gathered during ongoing sales and product reviews typically leads a company back to the beginning of the product development process.

PRODUCT PROMOTION

After a company has developed a product, the company's marketers and salespersons must successfully promote the product to generate consumer interest before any sales can take place. Marketers generally employ four promotional tools to help generate interest in a product: personal selling, advertising, sales promotion, and publicity.

Personal Selling

Personal selling is a promotional tool that relies on salespersons to present product information during face-to-face meetings with one or more prospective buyers. Figure 9-3 lists the typical elements of a personal sales presentation. Keep in mind that the entire process may require more than one meeting with a prospective buyer.

Personal selling is a primary promotional tool for insurers because it is one of the best means of communicating information about complex financial products such as annuities. However, personal selling is expensive, and insurers do not generally use it when they want to reach large numbers of potential customers.

FIGURE 9.3

Personal Sales Presentation for an Annuity.

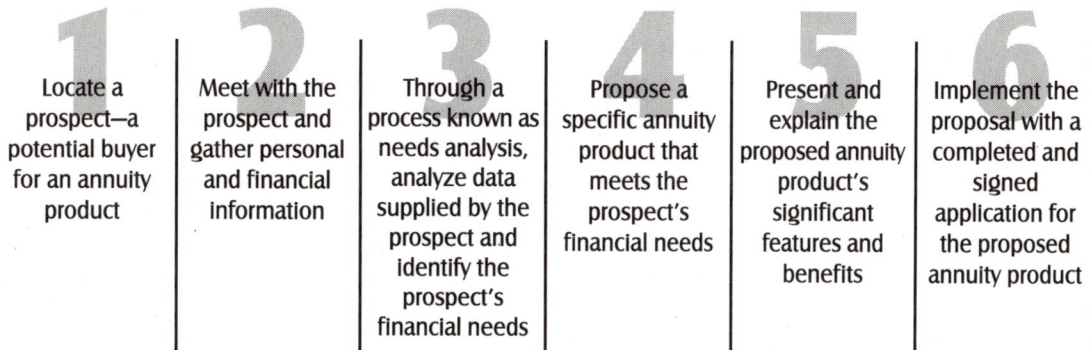

1	2	3	4	5	6
Locate a prospect—a potential buyer for an annuity product	Meet with the prospect and gather personal and financial information	Through a process known as needs analysis, analyze data supplied by the prospect and identify the prospect's financial needs	Propose a specific annuity product that meets the prospect's financial needs	Present and explain the proposed annuity product's significant features and benefits	Implement the proposal with a completed and signed application for the proposed annuity product

Advertising

Advertising is a form of promotion that provides information about a company or its products and services. Advertising is generated by an identified sponsor and transmitted, for a fee, by the mass media—television, radio, direct mail, newspapers, and magazines—and outdoor media—billboards, signs, and posters. The Internet is also fast becoming a prime location for product advertising and promotion. Advertising is more economical than personal selling because it allows the insurer to reach large numbers of potential customers at a much lower cost. However, insurers must choose advertising media carefully to ensure that advertisements appear in media that will be seen by consumers in the insurers' target markets.

Sales Promotion

A *sales promotion* is a type of incentive that a company offers to encourage salespersons to sell a product or to encourage consumers to purchase a product. For example, insurers may sponsor sales contests offering cash prizes, merchandise, or other incentives to salespersons who sell its products. To encourage customers to buy its products, an insurer might engage in *specialty advertising*, which is a form of consumer sales promotion that uses articles imprinted with a company name or logo, address, phone number, and sometimes a sales message to promote the company, its salespeople, or its products. These imprinted articles typically include items such as calendars, coffee mugs, and pens. Most sales promotion efforts are short-term and intended to spur sales during a defined period. Insurers often use sales promotions in connection with the release of new or revised products.

Publicity

Publicity is a form of promotion that provides information about a company or its products and services, and is transmitted in a news format by the mass media. Unlike advertising, with publicity the insurer neither pays to present the information nor generates or controls the message the media delivers. Because the insurer incurs no direct cost for publicity, it is one of the most economical means of getting company and product information to consumers and distributors. In addition, the information is often presented in a news format and so may be considered more credible than a company-sponsored advertisement. However, an insurer cannot guarantee how, or if, the media will cover a particular product or event. Publicity can be either positive or negative.

In addition to the promotional tools mentioned above, insurers typically develop extensive marketing materials—including brochures, sales illustrations, and informative guides—to help promote interest in annuity products and encourage sales. Most marketing materials focus on the appropriate uses of annuities, how annuities work, and the specific features contained in various types of annuity contracts. Figure 9-4 provides an overview of annuity uses and product features that are often included in annuity sales promotions, advertisements, and marketing materials. We have discussed these uses and features in detail throughout the text.

FIGURE 9.4

Annuity Uses and Product Features.

Annuity Uses	Product Features
Retirement savings	Tax-deferred wealth accumulation
Individual annuities	Variety of annuity payout options
Group annuities	Potential for a guaranteed lifetime income
Education savings	Death benefit guarantees
Managing lump sum cash distributions	Fixed annuity interest rate guarantees
Pensions	Variable annuity investment options
Insurance settlements	
Gifts	

DISTRIBUTION SYSTEMS

Now that you have seen the various promotional tools available to insurers, let's take a closer look at how insurers distribute annuity products to consumers. A **distribution system**, also called a *distribution channel*, is a method of transferring products from a manufacturer—in this case an insurance company—to consumers. Insurance companies use a variety of distribution systems to market annuities. However, these distribution systems typically fall into two general categories.

♦ A **personal selling distribution system** is a sales distribution system that uses commissioned or salaried salespersons to sell products through oral and written presentations to consumers. Salespersons and consumers have face-to-face contact with one another during the sales process.

◆ A ***direct response distribution system*** is a sales distribution system wherein the consumer purchases products directly from a company by responding to the company's advertisements or telephone solicitations. No face-to-face contact occurs between consumers and company salespersons during the sales process.

Personal Selling Distribution Systems

Because annuities are complex financial products, insurance companies have traditionally relied on personal selling by salespersons, who can explain the appropriate uses, provisions, and tax advantages of annuities to prospective buyers. Insight 9-1 emphasizes the advantages of personal selling for certain types of annuity products.

INSIGHT 9.1   **Personal Selling for Equity-Indexed and Market Value Adjusted Annuities.**

In recent years, many insurers have stepped up efforts to market their products through direct response distribution systems. However, some insurance and annuity products remain too complex for easy sales through these channels.

For example, insurers typically use personal selling techniques to market equity-indexed annuities and market value adjusted annuities. The calculations used to arrive at values for these products are extremely complex and not easily explained or understood. And, as we mentioned in Chapter 8, there is considerable uncertainty regarding whether these particular annuity products should be subject to federal securities regulation in the United States.

Further, the unique features of equity-indexed annuities and market value adjusted annuities can cause consumer interest in these products to fluctuate in relation to prevailing economic conditions. As a result of these factors, in many cases, a personal sales presentation is the most effective way for an insurer to market and sell these types of annuity products.

In a personal selling distribution system, the salesperson is crucial to the success of the insurer's marketing programs. Therefore, many companies devote a great deal of time to developing strong relationships with the members of their sales force. In many cases, in addition to obtaining the appropriate licenses to market and sell annuity products, salespersons must enter into an agency contract with an insurer. An ***agency contract*** is a legal agreement whereby one party, known as the ***agent***, is authorized to perform certain acts for another party, known as the ***principal***. Under an agency contract, the insurer, who is the principal, authorizes the salesperson, who is the agent, to act on its behalf in distributing its products.

To market annuity and other insurance products, insurers have typically established one of three types of personal selling distribution systems.

◆ Agency building systems
◆ Nonagency building systems
◆ Broker-dealer relationships

Agency Building Systems

In general, companies that use an *agency building system* recruit and train their salespeople, and provide them with financial support and office facilities. Four common forms of agency building distribution systems insurers use to market annuity products include the ordinary agency system, the multiple-line agency (MLA) system, the salaried sales distribution system, and the location selling distribution system. We briefly describe each of these distribution systems below.

Ordinary Agency System. One of the most common forms of agency building systems is the *ordinary agency system*, which is a distribution system that uses full-time career agents and agent-brokers to sell and deliver insurance and annuity products. A *career agent* is a salesperson who is under contract to at least one insurance company. Most career agents are considered to be independent contractors, rather than employees of an insurance company.

Although career agents, by definition, are salespersons who hold an agency contract with at least one primary insurance company, most career agents are not under exclusive contract with that company. A career agent who places business with more than one insurance company is called an *agent-broker*. For the remainder of our discussion, we will use the term *sales agent* when referring collectively to career agents and agent-brokers. A sales agent's responsibilities include soliciting applications for new business, collecting initial premiums, and providing certain services to contract owners. Typically, compensation for sales agents is provided in the form of commissions. A *commission* is a type of payment for a sales agent's services that is usually based on a specified percentage of the premiums paid on each contract the agent sells.

The ordinary agency system can be subdivided into the branch office system and the general agency system. Under the *branch office system*, an insurance company establishes and maintains field sales offices. Each field sales office is headed by a *branch manager* who recruits, selects, and trains career agents and acts as the sales manager for the geographic area covered by the sales office. Generally, branch managers—who are compensated in the form of a salary—are not actively involved in selling the insurer's products. Under the branch office system, the insurance company employs the branch manager and all administrative personnel. The career agents who work in a branch office are under contract to the insurance company, not to the branch manager.

Under the *general agency system*, general agents establish and maintain field sales offices for the insurance company. A *general agent* is an independent business person who is under contract to the insurance company and is given the power to represent the insurance company and to develop new business within a geographically defined area. General agents receive a commission on all sales generated by the field sales office and often are actively involved in product sales. Career agents in the field sales office may be under contract to the general agent or to the insurance company; the administrative staff are employees of the general agent.

Multiple-Line Agency (MLA) System. As an alternative to the ordinary agency system, insurers can establish a more comprehensive type of agency distribution system. The *multiple-line agency (MLA) system* is a distribution system that uses career agents to market all of the life, health, annuity, and property/casualty products offered by groups of financially interrelated or commonly managed insurance companies. In contrast, when a life insurer establishes a traditional general agency distribution system, sales agents under contract to the insurer can sell the insurer's life and annuity products, but they cannot sell homeowner's insurance policies offered by an affiliated property/casualty provider.

Salaried Sales Distribution System. In addition to the agency building systems we have already discussed, many insurers market products through a *salaried sales distribution system*, which is a distribution system that relies on the use of a company's salaried sales representatives to sell and service all types of insurance and annuity products. *Salaried sales representatives* are employees of the insurer and are paid on a salary basis—unlike sales agents who are paid on a commission basis. Most salaried sales representatives also receive incentive compensation based on their sales. Although salaried sales representatives can sell all types of insurance and annuity products, the salaried sales distribution system is most often used in the distribution of group insurance and annuity products.

Location Selling Distribution System. Finally, a number of insurers market products through a *location selling distribution system*, which is a distribution system wherein an insurer sets up an office or installs an information kiosk in a retail store, a shopping mall, or a bank or other financial institution in order to attract customers for insurance and annuity products. Because only insurance companies can issue annuities, in order to market annuity products through location selling distribution systems, insurers usually establish a formal distribution agreement with a participating store, bank, or financial institution.

At retail sites, the sales office is typically staffed by salaried sales representatives the insurer employs. The representatives who sell annuities and insurance products in banks or other financial institutions can be either sales agents affiliated with the insurance company or insurance-licensed employees of the bank or participating financial institution. Prior to 1995, insurance companies and national banks disagreed about which types of companies and people could sell annuities. The U.S. Supreme Court settled the dispute in its *NationsBank of N.C. v. Variable Annuity Life Insurance Company (VALIC)* decision. The Supreme Court's decision in this case cleared the way for banks to sell annuities, but did not grant to banks the authority to issue annuities. As a result of this decision, many banks have moved forward aggressively in their efforts to sell annuity products by establishing their own licensed insurance agencies or by entering into distribution agreements with established insurers.

Nonagency Building Systems

In general, companies that use a **nonagency building system** recruit salespeople who require little training, are financially self-supporting, and operate out of independent office facilities. The two most commonly used forms of nonagency building systems are the personal-producing general agency (PPGA) system and the brokerage system. We briefly describe these distribution systems below.

Personal-Producing General Agency (PPGA) System. A *personal-producing general agency (PPGA) system* is a distribution system that relies on personal-producing general agents to sell and deliver insurance and annuity products. A *personal-producing general agent* is a commissioned sales agent who typically works alone, is not housed in an insurance company field office, and engages primarily in personal selling. Typically, a personal-producing general agent is an experienced agent who requires little or no training. Personal-producing general agents often hold agency contracts with several insurers.

Brokerage Distribution System. A *brokerage distribution system* is a distribution system that relies on the use of agent-brokers and licensed brokers to sell and deliver insurance and annuity products. As we mentioned previously, an agent-broker is a career agent who places business with more than one insurance company. A *licensed broker* is a salesperson who is not under an agency contract with any insurance company and who is acting as an agent of the buyer.

Broker-Dealers

Insurance companies also can market products through another distribution channel—the broker-dealer. A *broker-dealer* is a firm that (1) provides information or advice to its customers regarding the sale and/or purchase of securities, (2) serves as a financial intermediary between buyers and sellers by underwriting or acquiring securities in order to market them to its customers, and (3) supervises the sales process to make sure that sales agents comply with applicable SEC and NASD regulations.

Because variable annuity products are considered securities in the United States, insurers can sell these products only through broker-dealer firms. Insurance companies can establish their own broker-dealer subsidiaries, or they can enter into relationships with existing broker-dealer firms.

Direct Response Distribution Systems

Under direct response distribution systems, insurance companies sell products through direct appeals to consumers in a variety of advertising media, including television, radio, newspapers, magazines, and Internet Web sites. Some companies also mail product information directly to consumers or make use of telephone sales solicitations to contact consumers at home.

Unlike the other types of distribution systems we have discussed, sales agents and consumers have no face-to-face contact with one another in a direct response distribution system. Product advertisements and other forms of direct response solicitation generally contain all the information that the consumer needs to make a purchase decision and to apply for the product. Direct response advertisements and solicitations typically include either (1) an application for the consumer to complete and return to the insurer or (2) instructions for the consumer to contact the insurer for an application or to obtain more information. Some insurance and annuity products are also available for purchase directly through insurance company Web sites on the Internet. Insight 9-2 examines one insurer's entry into the online sale of annuities.

INSIGHT 9.2

Cyberlaunch: Lincoln Designs a Variable Annuity for Web Sales.

Lincoln Financial Direct, Leesburg, Va., has launched a variable annuity to be sold exclusively through an Internet Web site, www.eannuity.com. The product, eAnnuity, is available to residents of 31 states, and sales began September 30, 1998.

It is the first variable annuity customers are able to buy without any human intervention, said Jon Boscia, chief executive officer of Lincoln National Corp., the Fort Wayne, Ind.-based parent of Lincoln Financial.

Its fees and expenses are among the lowest in the industry and are lower than those of the average stock mutual fund, Boscia said, thanks to the low-cost means of distribution.

The eAnnuity is designed for people comfortable with the Internet who already have self-directed buying habits, said Shane Chalke, vice president of Internet marketing for Lincoln and creator of the eAnnuity. Customer service is also online, including fund switching, changes of address, withdrawals, and deposits.

Source: Excerpted from Ron Panko, "Cyberlaunch: Lincoln Designs a Variable Annuity for Web Sales," *BestWeek*, Life/Health ed. (October 5, 1998): 2. Used with permission.

CHOOSING A DISTRIBUTION SYSTEM

Before deciding on a particular distribution system for its products, an insurer must evaluate the system's strengths and weaknesses in relation to the company's needs and the types of products it is marketing. Insurers must consider

- ◆ The characteristics of buyers in the target market, including the number of buyers, types of buyers, location of buyers, buyer's preferred ways of purchasing the products offered, and the complexity of buyers' needs.

- ◆ The types and complexity of products the company is selling. For example, complex products typically require personal selling. Direct marketing usually works best for selling uncomplicated, easy-to-understand products.

- ◆ The marketing environment in which the company operates, including current and projected economic conditions, technological advances, competitive forces, legal rulings, and social conditions.

- ◆ The characteristics of the company, including human, technological, and financial resources; the company's mission, goals, objectives, culture, and marketing philosophy; and the company's existing distribution channels.

- ◆ The degree of control the company desires to exercise over distribution systems. For example, company-owned distribution systems provide the greatest degree of control, but also are typically the most expensive to support.

KEY TERMS AND CONCEPTS

marketing
exchange
marketing mix
product
price
promotion
distribution
market
market segments
market segmentation
target marketing
target market
marketing plan
screening process
comprehensive business analysis
market analysis
product design objectives
personal selling
advertising
sales promotion
specialty advertising
publicity
distribution system
personal selling distribution system
direct response distribution system
agency contract
agent
principal
agency building system
ordinary agency system
career agent
agent-broker
commission
branch office system
branch manager
general agency system
general agent

multiple-line agency (MLA) system
salaried sales distribution system
salaried sales representative
location selling distribution system
nonagency building system
personal-producing general agency (PPGA) system
personal-producing general agent
brokerage distribution system
licensed broker
broker-dealer

CHAPTER 10

The Future of Annuities

After studying this chapter, you should be able to

◆ Discuss societal changes that may affect the annuities industry

◆ Discuss changes to Social Security that may affect the annuities industry

◆ Describe changes in employer-sponsored pension plans that may affect the annuities industry

◆ Discuss tax and regulation issues that may have an impact on the annuities industry

◆ Describe how insurers are responding to change and the role that annuities may play as change occurs in society and in the financial services industry

As we have indicated throughout the text, the types of annuities that consumers purchase, whether annuity sales increase or decline, and how insurers react to the changing environment all can differ dramatically, depending upon a variety of factors. In this chapter, we will discuss several of these factors and how changes in these factors might affect the annuities industry. We will discuss developments in American society, proposals regarding Social Security, changes in employer-sponsored pension plans, changes in the taxation and regulation of annuities, the role annuities might play as change occurs, and how insurers are adapting marketing and product development strategies to respond to these changes.

SOCIETAL DEVELOPMENTS

In recent years, attitudes regarding personal responsibility have changed. Americans from different economic, ethnic, and age groups are being urged to depend more upon their own resources for needs ranging from college tuition costs to retirement income. Although numerous government and private programs to assist people do exist, in many cases, program resources have been reduced. In addition, many people are reluctant to turn to family members in times of need. So a number of people approaching retirement age may not be able to rely upon the government or their families to the same extent that previous generations could. Consequently, many people express concern about how they will support themselves in retirement. Insight 10-1 discusses the confidence Americans have about their financial preparations for retirement.

Growing Number of Retirees

Without a doubt the most important societal change that will affect the annuities industry will be the increase in the number of people entering retirement. Within the next 30 years, the number of people in the U.S. population over age 65 will double. Unless something is done now, some experts predict that by the year 2030 the Social Security system will be unable to provide its current level of benefits to this growing number of retirees. As the chart in Figure 10-1 indicates, Old-Age, Survivors and Disability Insurance (OASDI), popularly known as "Social Security," accounts for a significant portion of the annual income of those over age 65.

Although Social Security payments were never intended to be a large percentage of income for retirees, Figure 10-1 is an indication of how important those payments have become.

INSIGHT 10.1

Results of the 1998 Retirement Confidence Survey.

The boom times of the 1990s are an apparent bust when it comes to increasing Americans' retirement confidence, according to the results of the 1998 Retirement Confidence Survey (RCS) co-sponsored by the Employee Benefit Research Institute (EBRI), the American Savings Education Council (ASEC), and Mathew Greenwald & Associates (MGA). The reason may be that more Americans have tried to figure out how much money they really need to save—and the answers have them worried.

A consistent 20 to 25 percent of working Americans are very confident that they will have enough money to live comfortably through their retirement years. This figure has remained within this range over a period that includes some of the most prosperous years in this century.

According to EBRI President Dallas Salisbury, increasing numbers of every age group have tried to figure out how much they need to save by retirement. Forty-five percent of working Americans have made the calculation, up from 32 percent in 1996 and 36 percent in 1997. The increase is particularly striking among baby boomers. Half of the older boomers (those born between 1946–1953) have now tried to figure out what they'll need.

"More and more Americans—especially the baby boomer generation—are recognizing that they may be retired for 20 or more years, and are trying to figure out what a retirement that long will cost. When we ask them about specific retirement costs, we can see their worries increasing," noted MGA President Mathew Greenwald.

Half of workers (51 percent) are worried they won't have enough money for long-term health care. More than one-third are worried they will not be able to take care of medical expenses, and 30 percent—almost one-third—don't think they will have enough money to support themselves in retirement no matter how long they live.

Concern remains about the nearly one-third of Americans who are not saving and the reasons they don't. According to the RCS, most think they are already stretched to the limit. Almost 50 percent of nonsavers cite "too many current financial responsibilities" as the most important reason they don't save, with 66 percent indicating it is a major reason. Yet both savers and nonsavers agree they could save an additional $20 a week.

Fear seems to be an important motivator in encouraging workers to save. "Seeing people not prepare and struggle" (48 percent) and "time running out" (37 percent) are the first and second strongest motivators people cite for starting to save. This perception may in fact reflect reality. Among retirees, 20 percent indicate that their standard of living has been worse than expected.

Source: Adapted from "Boom Times A Bust for Retirement Assurances: Results of the 1998 Retirement Confidence Survey," *EBRI Online* 2 June 1998, http://www.ebri.org/sers/pr417/htm (19 June 1998). Used with permission.

FIGURE 10.1

Annual Income of Elderly Individuals (Ages 65 and Older) from Specified Sources, by Income Quintile, 1996.

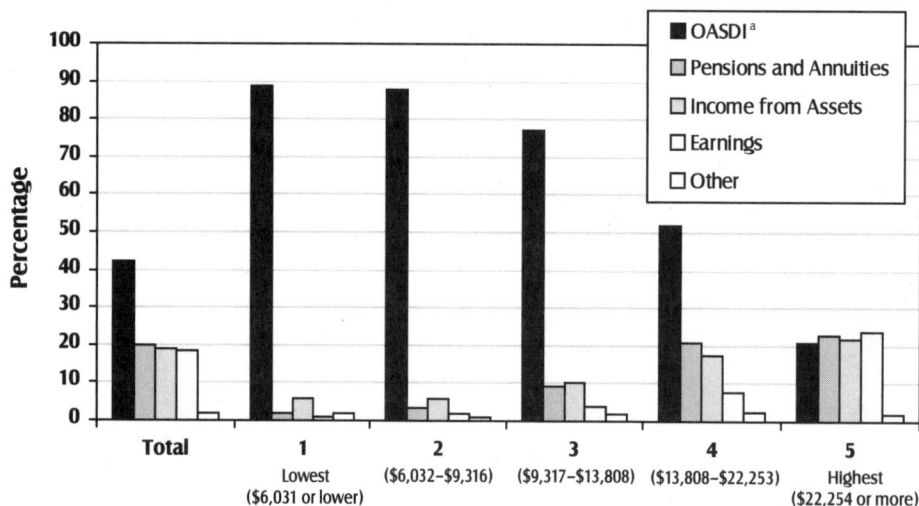

Legend: OASDI[a] · Pensions and Annuities · Income from Assets · Earnings · Other

Y-axis: Percentage (0–100)

X-axis categories:
- Total
- 1 Lowest ($6,031 or lower)
- 2 ($6,032–$9,316)
- 3 ($9,317–$13,808)
- 4 ($13,808–$22,253)
- 5 Highest ($22,254 or more)

[a]Old-Age, Survivors and Disability Insurance

Source: Employee Benefit Research Institute tabulations of the March 1996 Current Population Survey. Used with permission.

Lengthening of Retirement

Not only is the number of retirees growing, but the length of their retirements is increasing as well. In the past, retirees spent 5 to 10 years in retirement. Today, especially in cases where people retire as early as age 55, some retirees may find that the length of their retirement is as long as or longer than their working years. Retirement periods that last 20 or 30 years require a dramatic increase in the resources available to fund the lengthy periods that people will spend out of the workforce. In fact, as Insight 10-2 suggests, financial planners can break retirement into distinctive phases to help their clients plan for the financial realities of retirement.

INSIGHT 10.2   ## Planning for a "Three-Phase" Retirement.

There was a time when retirement meant sitting on a porch, smoking a pipe, waving at young children and waiting to die. Well, that's changed, said Michael Stein, speaking at this year's College for Financial Planning. No longer is retirement a gloomy five-year period before death, but a time of adventure that often lasts for decades, he said.

Presenting "The Three-Phase Retirement: Key to the Prosperous Retirement," Mr. Stein said today's retirees are the healthiest, wealthiest, and most educated the world has ever seen. Citing U.S. census data, Mr. Stein said that in 1900 the average 65-year-old had a life expectancy of 11.86 years. Today that figure is 18.3 years, an increase of 54 percent, he said, and future projections say life expectancies will only get longer.

Given the increase, and the fact that many people aim to retire at a younger age, financial planners and retirees alike should no longer view retirement as one single homogeneous phase, he said. Instead, they should break it down into three distinct phases.

Phase one—"the active stage"—he described as the "go-go" phase, a second childhood, which for many people lasts until their mid-70s. Phase two is the "passive retirement phase"—a time when life starts becoming quieter and a little more introspective. Phase three—"the final phase"—is characterized by the need for medical and nursing care.

Planners should channel as much of their clients' financial resources into phase one without risking their future in the remaining phases, Mr. Stein said. Clients can enjoy the full fruits of the active phase when their retirement is mapped out in this manner, he said.

The active phase is often one of world trips, or the pursuit of expensive hobbies, he said. During the active phase—the most expensive of the three phases—a retiree's living expenses are often greater than in pre-retirement. The argument, Mr. Stein said, that an individual's expenses decrease at retirement is not true.

Planners should put in place two budgets for all three phases, Mr. Stein said. He called them the "active lifestyle budget" (which funds leisure activities, new cars, etc.) and the "subsistence" level budget, which covers the essentials such as food and housing. The active budget is typically 25 percent to 30 percent higher than the subsistence budget, he said.

Mr. Stein said that as the retiree moves closer to the final phase, the active lifestyle budget will typically get closer to the subsistence budget since the retiree's desire for expensive pursuits declines.

To successfully fund all three phases, planners need to adopt long-term investment strategies for their clients, he said, adding planners should steer clear in most cases of heavily weighting their clients' portfolios in bonds.

For example, in putting an asset allocation strategy in place for one of his 63-year-old clients, Mr. Stein used an asset allocation time horizon of 24½ years. Given that, his client's assets are heavily invested in equities, he said.

To generate the asset allocation figure of 24½, Mr. Stein used the following formula: Estimated Years until Death *plus* Average time to Capital Withdrawal, divided by two.

Mr. Stein estimated that his 63-year-old client has 31 years of life left, in line, statistically speaking, with between 10 percent to 20 percent of 63-year-olds right now. Additionally, he expects to start depleting the retiree's capital base in 18 years, given the client's current asset mix.

For retirees heavily invested in equities who fear a market correction, Mr. Stein assures their security with the subsistence budget.

He illustrated this with the following example. A client has a $100,000 yearly active lifestyle budget—$40,000 from pensions and Social Security, and $60,000 from a 6 percent return on a $1 million portfolio. Should the portfolio drop to $700,000, due to a major correction, Mr. Stein said, his client would now have an annual budget of $82,000, $42,000 (6 percent of $700,000) plus $40,000. This is still likely to be well above the subsistence budget, he said.

Mr. Stein also suggested that planners maximize tax-deferred vehicles. For healthy people in their late 50s and early 60s, tax deferral can still be extremely beneficial, he said.

For investment periods greater than 20 years, tax deferral is extremely advantageous in terms of wealth accumulation, he said. He added that planners, in providing income for their clients, should draw down on taxable accounts first.

SOCIAL SECURITY

During the past several years, a number of different people and organizations have subjected Social Security to close scrutiny and have concluded that it will need to change. Many groups and organizations are sponsoring research to determine the best way to reform Social Security. The Social Security Administration itself is funding a number of different projects. Insight 10-3 discusses one step the Social Security Administration has taken to deal with this situation.

INSIGHT 10.3

Social Security Reform Research Centers Named.

Boston College and the University of Michigan have been selected by the Social Security Administration to establish research centers to help set the agenda for reform of the nation's retirement system. Boston College will receive a five-year, $5.25 million grant from the Social Security Administration to establish a retirement policy research center based at the school's Carroll School of Management.

These are the first grants made through the Social Security Administration's Retirement Research Consortium program, and the funds will support research that will influence retirement policy decision making in both the public and private sectors. According to Social Security Commissioner Kenneth S. Apfel, the new centers are a crucial element in the Social Security Administration's strategy for meeting the future retirement needs of Americans.

The grants were awarded on the basis of the recommendations of an expert review panel. The universities will host a joint conference on retirement.

Source: Excerpted from "Social Security Reform Research Centers Named," *Best's Review,* Life/Health ed. (December 1998): 93. Used with permission.

Numerous legislators, policy makers, and public and private groups have proposed methods for changing Social Security. These proposals range from modifying Social Security to eventually eliminating it. In all likelihood, over the next several years some combination of the following changes will be implemented:

◆ Modifying Social Security

◆ Establishing individual savings or personal retirement accounts

◆ Phasing out Social Security

Modifying Social Security

Many proposals call for making changes to the current Social Security system. Supporters of this approach believe that raising the age at which benefits can begin, reducing benefits slightly, and raising the amount of salary income subject to Social Security taxes will be sufficient.

Establishing Individual Savings or Personal Retirement Accounts

A number of other proposals call for establishing some type of individual savings or personal retirement account for each worker who currently contributes to Social Security. Although the proposals differ in the percent to be contributed and how the accounts would be managed, they all generally call for depositing 1–2 percent of a person's current Social Security contribution into an individual account. One such plan views this type of personal or individual account as a supplement to Social Security and would fund the individual accounts with anticipated federal budget surpluses. Other plans would take the 1–2 percent contribution from Social Security taxes and reduce Social Security benefits.

Phasing Out Social Security

Although a proposal to abolish Social Security altogether is unlikely, a number of critics contend that, for future retirees, the private sector could do a much better job of meeting retirement needs. Many feel that if people were able to invest their payroll taxes on their own in individual accounts, they would be able to accumulate far more than they are likely to receive in Social Security benefits. However, any effort to phase out Social Security and replace it with private retirement accounts would be a decades-long process because of the need to ensure that current Social Security recipients and those who soon will be able to receive benefits would not be penalized.

EMPLOYER-SPONSORED PENSION PLANS

The shift from defined benefit pension plans to defined contribution pension plans is likely to continue. As companies cut expenses in an increasingly competitive global business environment, employers are likely to ask employees to contribute a larger percentage of the total amount contributed to employer-sponsored retirement savings plans.

Encouraging 401(k) Participation

Most businesses with 401(k) plans simply inform employees that they are eligible to participate. The human resources department usually provides employees with educational materials about the 401(k) plan and may even sponsor seminars. However, even though the employer may contribute a percentage to match the employee's contribution, many employees still do not take advantage of their employer's 401(k) plan.

In 1998, the IRS ruled on an approach that some businesses have employed to encourage employees to contribute to employer-sponsored retirement plans. The IRS ruled that these businesses could automatically enroll employees, rather than make enrollment optional, dependent upon the employee's action. Under this alternative, the IRS ruled that employees must have the option to receive the contribution in cash, instead of having it contributed to the 401(k) plan. Insight 10-4 describes how two well-known companies have used automatic 401(k) enrollment.

Small Businesses

Small businesses frequently do not provide a retirement plan for employees. On the front page of the June 2, 1998, edition of the *Wall Street Journal*,

INSIGHT 10.4

McDonald's, J.C. Penney Try Automatic 401(k) Enrollment.

Some employers that have tried, but failed, to get employees to enroll in their 401(k) retirement savings plans have taken one last step to increase participation: make them join. A group of about 50 companies nationwide have adopted policies in which new hires are automatically enrolled in 401(k) plans unless they specifically refuse.

Participation in the 401(k) plan at J.C. Penney Co. of Plano, Texas, jumped to 89 percent of its 257,000 employees, from the low 70s, when the retailer launched its automatic enrollment plan a year ago, said Duncan Muir, a spokesperson.

H.J. Heinz Co. has had an automatic 401(k) enrollment policy since 1992. It applies to 5,000 employees.

A new employee enters the Heinz 401(k) the first day on the job, said Gary Matson, director of human resource services for Heinz. The company takes 3 percent of the employee's pretax salary, matches it dollar-for-dollar, and invests it in an array of mutual funds.

Workers who actively enroll in a 401(k) choose from a wide range of mutual funds, each with varying degrees of risk. In the absence of direction from an employee who is automatically enrolled, Heinz plays it safe.

"We put them in conservative, fairly stable funds so they are not exposed to a whole lot of risk," Matson said.

Once enrolled, employees have the option of increasing their contribution and moving their dollars from one investment vehicle to another within the plan. They also have the option of withdrawing from the plan altogether.

Source: Excerpted from Robert Mullins, "McDonald's, J.C. Penney Try Automatic 401(k) Enrollment," *Atlanta Business Chronicle* 11 to 17 December 1998, 3B. Used with permission.

Albert R. Karr in "Work Week" described a survey of 601 firms by the Employee Benefit Research Institute. Fifty percent of employers who responded to the survey said they do not have a retirement plan for their workers because company revenues are uncertain or employees prefer higher wages or other benefits. The same survey found that over two-thirds of small-business workers aren't covered by a retirement plan.

Many small-business owners do not want to incur the administrative costs of establishing a retirement savings plan for their employees. However, they may be unaware of retirement savings plans that cost less to administer, such as the SEP and SIMPLE plans that we discussed in Chapter 6. As the employer's role in helping employees prepare for retirement gains more attention, public interest groups, government agencies, and employees of small businesses are likely to increase their efforts to inform small-business owners about retirement planning options for employees and to encourage them to establish retirement savings plans. Because many of these business owners have not established their own retirement savings plans, both they and their employees could benefit from these efforts.

TAX REFORM AND THE REGULATION OF ANNUITIES

At any point in time, proposals for federal and state legislation regarding the taxation and regulation of annuities can be found at some stage in the legislative process. However, in the past, many of these proposals never made it out of the committees that recommend the items legislators will vote on. And many proposals that were voted upon were not enacted. Such has been the case with some of the most highly publicized proposed legislation of recent years. In addition, if a piece of legislation is enacted at some point in time, it might be reversed in the future.

Proposals to Tax 1035 Exchanges

As we mentioned in Chapter 5, the tax-deferred status of earnings is one advantage annuities have over mutual funds. As you will recall, Section 1035 of the Internal Revenue Code allows owners of annuities to exchange one annuity contract for another without incurring current income taxes on earned income from the first contract. The U.S. Congress has debated whether to modify the 1035 exchange, so that annuity contract owners would be required to pay taxes on annuity earnings, if owners replaced one annuity contract with another annuity contract. Insurers and retirement planning experts have countered with the argument that such a move would only worsen the current poor status of savings habits in the United States. So far, this proposed change to the Internal Revenue Code has not been passed.

Changes in the Capital Gains Tax

In 1997, Congress enacted legislation that lowered the taxes on capital gains. Many in the annuities industry feared that, as a result of this legislation, variable annuities would lose much of their advantage over mutual funds. Because payouts from all types of annuities are taxed as ordinary income, the tax rate on annuity payouts potentially could be higher than the capital gains paid on earnings from a mutual fund. But, as we mentioned earlier, earnings in a variable annuity are tax-deferred, while earnings in a mutual fund are not. Therefore, the after-tax value of the annuity payments might still be greater than the after-tax value of the mutual fund, depending on the tax status of the owner and the type of securities purchased. And, despite the lowering of the capital gains tax on mutual funds, variable annuity sales have continued to set records, with industry experts predicting that sales of variable annuities will continue to grow.

Regulation of Annuities

In Chapter 8, we discussed a number of the regulations that govern the annuities industry. Although the majority of those regulations have been in place for a number of years, the federal government and state agencies can enact new legislation to regulate the annuities industry at any time. In addition, state insurance departments have differed in their views of certain annuity products.

For example, state insurance departments and the SEC are likely to continue their close scrutiny of equity-indexed annuities. Some state insurance departments have classified equity-indexed annuities as fixed products, while others have classified them as variable products. As we mentioned in Chapter 8, such a difference in classification dramatically affects how insurers market and sell equity-indexed annuities. To avoid any potential problems, a number of insurers have designed their equity-indexed annuities so that they are clearly variable products that must be registered with the SEC and that must be sold by people registered with the NASD.

However, as we mentioned in Chapter 8, other insurers successfully have argued that their equity-indexed annuities should be regulated as fixed products, which do not require registration of the product with the SEC.

POTENTIAL EFFECTS OF CHANGE ON ANNUITIES

As one might expect, any move towards encouraging people to take more responsibility for guaranteeing their own retirement income is bound to create an interest in individual and group annuities.

As Insight 10-1 mentioned, many people are worried that they have not saved enough to provide for a comfortable retirement. Whether that worry translates into increased rates of saving may depend upon efforts to educate the American public about the need for retirement savings. Insurers and other financial services institutions have an opportunity to help provide that education.

Social Security and Annuities

If the U.S. Congress passes legislation to establish individual retirement accounts for all working Americans, a very diverse group of people would then need financial planning advice. Insurers currently provide individual and group annuities to millions of Americans. Because insurers have established a reputation for careful handling of the funds entrusted to them, some would say they are one of the logical choices for providing government-established accounts. Insurers also offer a wide variety of annuity products that may be able to meet the very different needs of such a diverse group.

Employer-Sponsored Retirement Plans and Annuities

Perhaps the most obvious place for educational efforts to encourage increased retirement saving is in the workplace. Many insurance companies already distribute numerous retirement planning publications to employees in group retirement plans or provide Web sites where those employees can get information about 401(k), 403(b), and other types of employer-sponsored retirement plans.

However, insurers may want to consider expanding their educational efforts to include informing their group clients about automatic 401(k) enrollment. As Insight 10-4 mentioned, companies that have established automatic enrollment have had dramatic increases in the number of employees participating in their 401(k) plans.

In addition, as we have already pointed out, many small businesses have not established any type of retirement plan, because they are wary of the complexities and costs.

How Insurers Respond to Change Through Product Design and Marketing

Although opportunities for sales of their annuity products are increasing, insurers also face increasing competition from other financial services companies. To respond to the changes taking place in society and in the financial services industry, insurers recently have added new product features to their annuities. Insurers are also looking at new ways to market their annuities.

Variable Annuity Charges

One way insurers are making their variable annuity products more competitive is through the reduction and even elimination of the usual variable annuity charges and fees. Several insurers have recently eliminated these types of charges and fees.

Flexible Provisions

Insurers are designing products that give contract owners more flexibility. Some insurers have added terminal illness benefit and nursing home benefit provisions to their deferred annuity contracts. These provisions typically state that a lump sum withdrawal of up to 100 percent of the contract value can be withdrawn without any surrender charge. One reason that many annuity contract owners have chosen a lump sum withdrawal over a payout option is a reluctance to lose control over principal. These contract owners want the security of knowing that they can get to their money in case of an emergency. For that reason, some insurers have added a **commutation right** to payout options, which states that the contract owner can withdraw a lump sum from the contract's remaining principal—and any growth of the principal of a variable contract—even if the contract owner is receiving annuity payments. However, if a contract owner chooses to exercise the commutation right, the lump sum payment will reduce the present value of the contract, which will reduce the amount of future annuity payments.

As described in Insight 10-5, one insurer has introduced a variable annuity whose features can be adjusted during the life of the contract.

INSIGHT 10.5 **Aetna Gives Investors Right to Adjust Variable Annuities.**

Aetna Life Insurance and Annuity Co., Hartford, Conn., has introduced Aetna Variable Annuity, which lets investors adjust certain features over the life of the contract without incurring surrender charges.

Offered through Aetna Retirement Services, the product includes invest-ment options from well-known fund families, fixed investment options, dollar cost averaging, account rebalancing, and both fixed- and variable-annuitization options. But Aetna says the ability to adjust product features is unique in the industry. Owners may change the minimum initial deposit, withdrawal options, and death-benefit provisions. They may also elect a nursing-care waiver.

The Aetna Variable Annuity is distributed through third-party intermediaries such as financial planners, banks, brokers, and other financial institutions.

Source: Reprinted from "Aetna Gives Investors Right to Adjust Variable Annuities," *Best's Review,* Life/Health ed. (December 1998): 86. Used with permission.

Encouraging Annuitization

As we mentioned earlier in the text, only a very small percentage of annuity contract owners choose a life annuity payout option. One way for insurers to provide an added benefit for contract owners and to retain management of contract owners' funds is to encourage annuitization. After all, annuities were intended not only to be a tax-deferred way to accumulate retirement savings, but also to provide an income that the contract owner would not outlive. Many industry experts believe that if insurers provide information about the benefits of annuitization, more contract owners may choose this option in the future.

Direct Marketing and the Internet

Personal selling by agents has been the traditional method for selling annuities. Because annuities—especially variable annuities—are complex products, insurers believed that an agent or representative needed to be available to answer buyer questions or explain contract provisions. But, as we have indicated elsewhere in this text, today's buyers of financial services products are more comfortable with the complexities of investment products, as evidenced by the number of Americans who purchase mutual funds directly from mutual fund companies. In addition, increasing numbers of people are buying and selling stocks using online discount brokerages. Insight 10-6 describes some of the characteristics of tomorrow's annuity buyer.

INSIGHT 10.6

A Guessing Game: Will Fading Distribution Systems Slow Down Annuity Sales?

Over the past 10 years, customers and their needs have changed. Annuity writers have responded to these changes by enhancing existing products and developing new products and features—changes that have included updated variable products, the introduction of equity-indexed annuities, and improvements to immediate annuities. Coupled with the right combination of agents, banks, stockbrokers, and direct marketers, annuity sales have averaged double-digit growth for over a decade.

While the past decade has focused on product development, the next decade could bring major changes in distribution systems. Consumers are changing how they purchase financial products, and companies will have to respond to these changes. Compared to today's annuity buyer, tomorrow's buyer will be

♦ Less likely to have a relationship with a life insurance agent
♦ Less likely to have a relationship with a bank representative
♦ Less likely to do business with a

commission-based financial services representative
♦ More likely to use a fee-based financial planner
♦ More comfortable with receiving information online
♦ More likely to purchase financial products directly from a company
♦ More likely to need retirement income protection
♦ As likely, if not more likely, to need advice on financial planning issues

Source: Excerpted from J. Scott Dunn, CLU, "A Guessing Game: Will Fading Distribution Systems Slow Down Annuity Sales?" *LIMRA's MarketFacts* (May/June 1998): 32. Used with permission.

And, as we discussed in Chapter 9, at least one insurer has designed an annuity for sale solely on the Internet. If Internet sales of other products are any indication, the potential market for selling financial products online is great. Consumers who express their preference for buying products online cite convenience and speed as reasons for making online purchases. Of course, a major difference between annuities and other financial products is the time commitment that a purchaser makes. Perhaps because the purchase of an annuity usually requires a commitment of several years and may involve considerable sums, purchasers of annuities still will prefer to deal with a financial services professional face-to-face.

KEY TERMS AND CONCEPTS

commutation right

APPENDIX

Sample Annuity Contract

ABC Life Insurance Company

FLEXIBLE PREMIUM RETIREMENT ANNUITY

Contract Number   MI0099999

Annuitant   JOHN DOE

Contract Date   01-01-95

This policy is written to be easily understood. The words "we," "us" and "our" refer to ABC Life Insurance Company. We may use "you" or "yours" in reference to the Owner of this contract.

This contract is issued in consideration of the application and payment of the Initial Premium. Additional premiums may be paid as provided in the Premium Section. The Initial Premium is at least $50.00.

We agree to pay a Retirement Life Income to the Annuitant, if living on the Retirement Date. We also agree to pay a death benefit to the Beneficiary when we receive due proof that the Annuitant's death occurred before the Retirement Date.

The Retirement Life Income is payable monthly unless less frequent payments are elected by the Owner. The death benefit is the Accumulation Value.

These payments and any other contractual benefits are subject to the terms of this contract which are contained on this and the following pages.

For service or information on this contract, contact our agent, agency office or our Home Office.

NOTICE OF TEN-DAY RIGHT TO EXAMINE CONTRACT
You may, within 10 days after receipt of this Contract, return it to Us, or to the agent who sold it, along with a written request for cancellation, whereupon any premium paid will be refunded in full and the Contract shall be void from the Effective Date with You and the Company being in the same position as if no Contract had been executed.

Signed for ABC LIFE INSURANCE COMPANY at its Home Office in Bloomington, Illinois.

Heather R. King
Secretary

B.J. Nemitt
President

_____
Registrar

Retirement Income on Retirement Date.
Premiums payable to Retirement Date.
Contract is non-participating.

CONTRACT SPECIFICATIONS

CONTRACT NUMBER   MI0099999

ANNUITANT   JOHN DOE

CONTRACT DATE   01-01-95

INITIAL PREMIUM $0.00

OWNER AND BENEFICIARY   AS STATED IN APPLICATION, UNLESS
CHANGED BY ENDORSEMENT

CONTRACT CONTENTS

Page No.

Introduction to Contract .... COVER
Contract Specifications 1

SECTION I — GENERAL PROVISIONS

    1.   This is a Contract 4
    2.   Change or Waiver of Terms 4
    3.   Age 4
    4.   Misstatement of Age or Sex 4
    5.   Premium and Net Premium 4
    6.   Accumulation Value 4
    7.   Assignment and Transfer 5
    8.   Owner, Annuitant and Beneficiary 5
    9.   Payment of Death Benefits 5

SECTION II — NON-PARTICIPATION 6

SECTION III — SURRENDER PROVISIONS

    1.   Cash Surrender of Accumulation Value 7
    2.   Partial Withdrawal of Accumulation Value 7
    2.a Deferral of Payment of Withdrawal Values 7
    3.   Withdrawal Value 7

SECTION IV — SETTLEMENT OPTIONS

    Option 1 — Interest Payment Option 8
    Option 2 — Fixed Time Payment Option 8
    Option 3 — Lifetime Payment Option 9
    Option 4 — Fixed Amount Payment Option 10
    Option 5 — Joint Lifetime Payment Option 10

A copy of the Application for this contract and any Riders and Endorsements follow page 11.

SECTION I
GENERAL PROVISIONS

1. THIS IS A CONTRACT. This is a legal contract between the Owner and the Company. The entire contract includes the application and any attached riders and endorsements.

2. CHANGE OR WAIVER OF TERMS. No change or waiver of any terms will be valid unless it is in writing and signed by our President, Vice President, Secretary, Assistant Secretary, or Actuary.

3. AGE Age, as used in this contract to determine rates and benefits, means age on the last birthday.

4. MISSTATEMENT OF AGE OR SEX. Two questions in the application concern the Annuitant's age and sex. If either or both of these are not correct, all benefits and amounts payable under this contract will be what the premiums paid would have bought if the correct age and sex had been stated. Any overpayment we make because of misstatement of age or sex together with interest thereon at 4 1/2 percent per year compounded annually will be deducted from the current or next succeeding payment or payments under this contract.

Any underpayments made will be added to the next payment with interest at 4 1/2 percent per year compounded annually. We reserve the right to require proof of age and sex of the Annuitant before making or continuing annuity payments under this contract.

5. PREMIUM. Premiums may be paid during the lifetime of the Annuitant, and prior to the Retirement Date. Each premium after the first is payable at our Home Office or to our authorized agent. Upon request, a receipt signed by our President or Secretary will be given for any premium payment. Premium payments may be made as frequently or infrequently as is desired. They may be discontinued at any time.

We reserve the right to refuse a payment of less than $50. In addition, we reserve the right to refuse all or any part of any premium payment in excess of $10,000.00 in any contract year unless this contract is part of a Qualified Plan under the Internal Revenue Code and such larger contribution is allowed under such plan.

NET PREMIUM.

The net premium is defined as the premium paid, less any applicable premium taxes.

6. ACCUMULATION VALUE. The Accumulation Value of this contract will be determined as of any date before annuity payments begin by accumulating the net premium from the date we receive it in our Home Office to such date at an interest rate determined by the Company but not less than 4 1/2% compounded for each contract year less the accumulation at the same interest rate of any reduction in Accumulation Value resulting from partial withdrawals.

All values and benefits under this contract are not less than those required by the laws of the state in which this contract is delivered. Upon request, we will provide you a statement showing the current Accumulation Value.

Page 4

7. ASSIGNMENT AND TRANSFER.

If this contract is part of a Qualified Plan under the Internal Revenue Code, it may not be sold, assigned, transferred, discounted, or pledged as collateral for a loan or as security for the performance of any obligation, or for any other purpose to any person. However, if this contract is owned by a Trust or a Custodian or an Employer as part of a Qualified Plan, the Trust, Custodian, or Employer may assign ownership of this contract to the Annuitant. The transfer, assignment or exercise of any ownership rights under this contract shall be made by written notice and shall be effective only if received by the Company at its Home Office. When received, such transfer, assignment or exercise of ownership rights shall take effect as of the date such notice was exercised.

In no event shall the Company be prejudiced by any payment made or action taken inconsistent with this transfer, assignment, or exercise before receipt of such notice. The Company assumes no responsibility for the validity of any assignment. The rights of the Owner or any Beneficiary shall be subject to the rights of any Assignee on record at the Home Office of the Company.

8. OWNER, ANNUITANT AND BENEFICIARY.

The Owner is the person who owns the contract as shown on our records. The Annuitant is the person on whose life Retirement Life Income payments are based. The Annuitant may be the owner or someone else may be the Owner.

If the Issue Age of the Annuitant is less than 15 years, ownership shall vest in the Annuitant on the contract anniversary that is on or follows the Annuitant's 18th birthday, unless the contract is endorsed to provide otherwise. If the Owner and all contingent owners die prior to that anniversary, the Annuitant shall then become the Owner.

A Beneficiary is any person named on our records to receive death proceeds after the Annuitant dies. There may be different classes of Beneficiaries such as primary and secondary. These classes establish the order of payment. Secondary Beneficiaries will not receive benefits if Primary Beneficiaries are alive. There may be more than one Beneficiary in a class. If no Beneficiary survives the Annuitant, the Owner will be the Beneficiary and if the Owner is the Annuitant, the Annuitant's estate will be the Beneficiary.

The Owner may change ownership or change any Beneficiary while the Annuitant is living. To make a change, a written request, satisfactory to us, must be received at our Home Office. The change will take effect as of the date the request is signed, even if the Annuitant dies before we receive it. Each change will be subject to any payment we made or other action we took before receiving the request.

9. PAYMENT OF DEATH BENEFITS.

On or prior to the Retirement Date, the death benefit under this contract is the Accumulation Value. After the Retirement Date, the death benefit is determined by the Settlement Option elected on the Retirement Date. Without regard to any contractual provisions, the following will apply to the extent required by law for this contract to be treated as an annuity contract under Federal Statutes:

1. IN GENERAL. This contract provides that

   A) if any Owner of this contract dies on or after the Retirement Date and before the entire interest in this contract has been distributed, the remaining portion of such interest will be distributed at least as rapidly as under the method of distribution being used as of the date of the Owner's death, and

   B) if the Owner dies before the Retirement Date, the entire interest will be distributed within 5 years after the death of the Owner.

2. EXCEPTION FOR CERTAIN AMOUNTS PAYABLE OVER LIFE OF BENEFICIARY.

   A) If any portion of the Owner's interest is payable to (or for the benefit of) a designated beneficiary,

   B) such portion will be distributed (in accordance with regulations) over the life of such designated beneficiary (or over a period not extending beyond the life expectancy of such beneficiary), and

   C) such distributions begin not later than 1 year after the date of the Owner's death or such later date as the Secretary of the Treasury may by regulations prescribe,

   then for purposes of paragraph (1), the portion referred to in subparagraph (A) shall be treated as distributed on the day on which such distributions begin.

3. SPECIAL RULE WHERE SURVIVING SPOUSE BENEFICIARY. If the designated beneficiary referred to in paragraph (2)(A) is the surviving spouse of the Owner of the contract, paragraphs (1) and (2) shall be applied by treating such spouse as the Owner of such contract.

4. DESIGNATED BENEFICIARY. For the purposes of this subsection, the term "designated beneficiary" means any individual designated a beneficiary by the Owner of the contract.

SECTION II
NON-PARTICIPATION

This contract is non-participating, its Premiums include no charge or consideration for participation in surplus.

SECTION III
SURRENDER PROVISIONS

1. CASH SURRENDER OF ACCUMULATION VALUE. At any time prior to the commencement of income and before the death of the Annuitant, you may elect to surrender the contract for the total withdrawal value described in Paragraph 3 below.

2. PARTIAL WITHDRAWAL OF ACCUMULATION VALUE. Partial withdrawals of Accumulation Value will be permitted. Partial withdrawals are limited to 4 per contract year and each such withdrawal shall not be less than $500 of Accumulation Value with the exception that if only 1 withdrawal is made in a contract year, it may be equal to 10% of the Accumulation Value as of the end of the previous contract year. With each such withdrawal, your written request is required and the contract must be submitted to the Home Office for endorsement. Partial withdrawals will reduce the Accumulation Value as described in Paragraph 3 below.

2.a DEFERRAL OF PAYMENT OF WITHDRAWAL VALUES. We may delay payment of any Accumulation Value or partial withdrawal thereof for up to six months after demand therefore.

3. WITHDRAWAL VALUE. The total withdrawal value is equal to your accumulation value times the withdrawal factor for the contract year in which your withdrawal is made.

In any contract year, you may withdraw an amount not greater than 10% of the Accumulation Value as of the end of the previous contract year and the withdrawal factor will be 1.00. Any amount withdrawn in excess of 10% will be divided by the withdrawal factor corresponding to the contract year in which the withdrawal is made, and the Accumulation Value will be further reduced by this result.

Contract Year of Withdrawal	Withdrawal Factor
1	.90
2	.91
3	.92
4	.93
5	.94
6	.95
7	.96
8	.97
9	.98
10	.99
11 & Over	1.00

If the withdrawal value is applied under settlement options 3 or 5 or determined at the time of the Annuitant's death prior to the commencement of income, then the withdrawal factor shall be 1.00.

If the withdrawal value is applied under settlement options 2 or 4, we will add the number of years in the term of the settlement option to the actual contract year of this contract to determine the withdrawal factor.

If the withdrawal value is applied under Settlement Option 1, the withdrawal factor at the date of settlement is 1.00. If proceeds left under Settlement Option 1 are subsequently withdrawn, we will apply a withdrawal factor determined by years elapsed from the Contract Date to the date such proceeds are withdrawn.

SECTION IV
SETTLEMENT OPTIONS

These are optional methods of settlement. They provide alternate ways in which payment can be made.

All or part of the Withdrawal Value of death benefit proceeds may be applied under any payment option. If this contract is assigned, any amount due to the assignee will be paid in one sum. The balance, if any, may be applied under any payment option.

If the amount to be applied under any option for any one person is less than $5,000, we may pay that amount in one sum instead. If the payments under any option come to less than $50 each, we have the right to make payments at less frequent intervals.

Our payment options are described below. Any other payment option agreed to by us may be elected. The payment options are described in terms of monthly payments. Annual, semiannual, or quarterly payments may be requested instead. The amount of these payments will be determined in a way which is consistent with monthly payments and will be quoted on request.

Option 1. Interest Payment Option. We will hold any amount applied under this option. Interest on the unpaid balance will be paid each month at a rate determined by us. This rate will not be less than the equivalent of 4% per year.

Option 2. Fixed Time Payment Option. Equal monthly payments will be made for any period selected, up to 30 years. The amount of each payment depends on the total amount applied, the period selected and the monthly payment rates we are using when the first payment is due. The rate of any payment will not be less than shown in the Option 2 Table.

OPTION 2 TABLE
Minimum Monthly Payment Rates for each $1,000 Applied

Years	Monthly Payment	Years	Monthly Payment
1	$84.84	16	$7.00
2	43.25	17	6.71
3	29.40	18	6.44
4	22.47	19	6.21
5	18.32	20	6.00
6	15.56	21	5.81
7	13.59	22	5.64
8	12.12	23	5.49
9	10.97	24	5.35
10	10.06	25	5.22
11	9.31	26	5.10
12	8.69	27	5.00
13	8.17	28	4.90
14	7.72	29	4.80
15	7.34	30	4.72

For quarterly payment, multiply by 2.990. For semiannual payment, multiply by 5.951. For annual payment, multiply by 11.787.

Option 3.   Lifetime Payment Option. Equal monthly payments are based on the life of a named person. Payments will continue for the lifetime of that person. The three variations are:

(A) Payments for life only. No specific number of payments is guaranteed. Payments stop when the named person dies.

(B) Payments guaranteed for amount applied. Payments stop when they equal the amount applied or when the named person dies, whichever is later.

(C) Payments guaranteed for 10, 15 or 20 years. Payments stop at the end of the selected guaranteed period or when the named person dies, whichever is later.

The Option 3 Table shows the minimum monthly payment for each $1,000 applied. The actual payments will be based on the monthly payment rates we are using when the first payment is due. They will not be less than shown in the Table.

OPTION 3 TABLE
Minimum Monthly Payment Rates for each $1,000 Applied

Age*	Payments For Life Only	Amount Applied	Payments Guaranteed For		
			10 Years	**15 Years**	**20 Years**
40	$4.13	$4.09	$4.12	$4.11	$4.09
45	4.36	4.29	4.34	4.32	4.28
50	4.65	4.54	4.62	4.58	4.52
55	5.05	4.87	4.99	4.91	4.81
60	5.56	5.30	5.45	5.32	5.14
65	6.27	5.87	6.07	5.82	5.48
70	7.33	6.65	6.89	6.38	5.76
75 & Over	8.95	7.74	7.89	6.87	5.92

*Age on birthday preceding the due date of the first payment. Monthly payment rates for ages not shown will be furnished on request. Monthly payment rates for ages over 75 are the same as those for 75.

Option 4.   Fixed Amount Payment Option. Each monthly payment will be for an agreed fixed amount. The amount of each payment may not be less than $10 for each $1,000 applied. Interest will be credited each month on the unpaid balance and added to it. This interest will be at a rate determined by us, but not less than the equivalent of 4% per year. Payments continue until the amount we hold runs out. The last payment will be for the balance only.

Option 5.   Joint Lifetime Payment Option. Equal monthly payments are based on the lives of two named persons. While both are living, one payment will be made each month. When one dies, the same payment will continue for the lifetime of the other.

The Option 5 Table shows the minimum monthly payment for each $1,000 applied. The actual payments will be based on the monthly payment rates we are using when the first payment is due. They will not be less than shown in the Table.

OPTION 5 TABLE
Minimum Monthly Payment Rates for each $1,000 Applied

Age of Second Payee*	Age of First Payee*					
	50	**55**	**60**	**65**	**70**	**75**
50	$4.21	$4.32	$4.41			
55	4.32	4.48	4.63	$4.75		
60	4.41	4.63	4.84	5.04	$5.21	
65		4.75	5.04	5.34	5.63	$5.86
70			5.21	5.63	6.07	6.49
75 & Over				5.86	6.49	7.16

*Age on birthday preceding the due date of the first payment. Monthly payment rates for ages not shown will be furnished on request. Monthly payment rates for ages over 75 are the same as those for 75.

To elect any option, we require that a written request, satisfactory to us, be received at our Home Office. The Owner may elect an Option during the Annuitant's lifetime. If the death benefit is payable in one sum when the Annuitant dies, the Beneficiary may elect an option with our consent.

Options for any amount payable to an association, corporation, partnership or fiduciary are available with our consent. However, a corporation or partnership may apply any amount payable to it under Option 3 or 5 if the option payments are based on the life or lives of the Annuitant, the Annuitant's spouse, any child of the Annuitant, or any other person agreed to by us.

The effective date of an option is the date the amount is applied under that option. For a death benefit, this is the date that due proof of the Annuitant's death is received at our Home Office. For the surrender value, it is the effective date of surrender.

The first payment is due on the effective date, except the first payment under Option 1 is due one month later. A later date for the first payment may be requested in the payment option election. All payment dates will f all on the same day of the month as the first one. No payment will become due until a payment date. No part payment will be made for any period shorter than the time between payment dates.

If provided in the payment option election, the following rights will be available:

> Under Options 1, 2, and 4, all or part of the unpaid balance may be withdrawn or applied under any other settlement option. The amount withdrawn or applied will be adjusted under the terms of the cancelled settlement agreement.

When computing the payments under Option 2, we include interest from the effective date of the option to the date of each payment. If future payments are withdrawn or paid early, we must deduct the amount of interest included for the period after withdrawal or early payment. The commuted value of future payments is the sum of those payments, less the interest from the date of withdrawal or early payment to the date of each future payment. The interest rate originally used in computing the option payments will be the rate used to determine the commuted value.

If the surrender value is applied under any option, we may delay payment of any withdrawal for up to six months.

To the extent permitted by law, each option payment and any withdrawal shall be free from legal process and the claim of any creditor of the person entitled to them. No option payment and no amount held under an option can be taken or assigned in advance of its payment date, unless the Owner's written consent is given before the Annuitant dies. This consent must be received at our Home Office.

GLOSSARY

Aa

401(k) plan. In the United States, an arrangement that allows both employers and employees to make contributions to a tax-deferred retirement savings plan established for the benefit of employees. [6]

403(b) plan. In the United States, an arrangement that allows not-for-profit employers and their employees to make contributions to a tax-deferred retirement savings plan established for the benefit of employees. [6]

457 plan. In the United States, an arrangement that allows state and local governments and their employees to make contributions to a tax-deferred retirement savings plan established for the benefit of employees. [6]

accumulated value. The net amount paid for an annuity plus interest earned, less the amount of any withdrawals or fees. [1]

accumulation period. The time period between the date that a contract owner purchases an annuity and the date that the payments begin. [1]

accumulation units. Units of measurement that represent ownership shares in the selected subaccount of a variable annuity. [2]

administrative fee. A fee charged by insurers to cover costs such as issuing a fixed or variable annuity, making administrative changes to the annuity contract, and preparing the contract owner's statement. In the case of some fixed annuity contracts, such fees are not charged separately but have been included in the premiums charged for the contract. [2]

advertising. A form of promotion that provides information about a company or its products and services; it is generated by an identified sponsor and transmitted, for a fee, by the mass media. [9]

after-tax dollars. Money after taxes have been paid on it. [7]

agency building system. A type of sales distribution system wherein companies generally recruit and train their salespeople, and provide them with financial support and office facilities. [9]

agency contract. A legal agreement whereby one party, known as the agent, is authorized to perform certain acts for another party, known as the principal. [9]

agent. A party that is authorized to perform certain acts for another party, known as the principal. [9]

agent-broker. A career agent who places business with more than one insurance company. [9]

AIR. *See* **assumed investment return.**

annual reset method. Also known as the *ratchet method.* A method for crediting excess interest to an equity-indexed annuity that involves comparing the value of the index at the start of the contract year with its value at the end of the contract year. The starting value is reset at the beginning of each contract year during the term of the contract. The insurer determines the amount of any index-based excess interest credit by averaging the results of each contract year of the contract term. [3]

Annual Return. In Canada, a financial report that contains detailed accounting and statistical data about an insurance company. [8]

Annual Statement. In the United States, a financial report containing detailed accounting and statistical data about an insurance company. [8]

annuitant. The person whose lifetime is used to measure the length of time annuity payments are payable under the annuity contract. [1]

annuitization. A payout option that involves payments tied to a life expectancy. [2]

annuity. A contract under which an insurance company promises to make a series of periodic payments to a named person in exchange for a premium or a series of premiums. [1]

annuity certain. An annuity that is payable for a stated period of time, regardless of whether the annuitant lives or dies. [2]

annuity contract. A legally enforceable written agreement under which an insurer promises to make a series of periodic payments to a named person, starting on a specified date, in exchange for a premium or series of premiums paid to the insurer. [1]

annuity date. *See* **income date.**

annuity period. The time span between each of the payments in a series of periodic annuity payments, typically either one month or one year. [1]

annuity units. Shares in an insurer's separate account that determine the size of future variable annuity payments after the income date has been reached. [4]

asset allocation. The process of investing funds proportionally in money markets, bonds, and stocks. [4]

asset allocation model. A tool that uses an investor's personal and financial data to generate options for strategically allocating investment funds. [4]

asset class. A group of similar investment instruments linked by related risk and return features. [4]

asset management fee. A fee charged on variable annuities by insurers to cover the management costs and operating expenses associated with the underlying investment funds. [2]

assignment provision. An annuity contract provision related to contract ownership that grants the nonqualified annuity contract owner the ability to temporarily or permanently transfer ownership of the contract. [2]

assumed investment return (AIR). The interest rate that variable annuity subaccount investments must earn in order for the annuity payment to remain the same throughout the payout period. [4]

automatic dollar cost averaging. A process whereby a variable annuity contract owner deposits premiums directly into a variable annuity's fixed account, money market subaccount, or other subaccount and then uses the funds to periodically purchase accumulation units in one or more of the annuity's other subaccounts. [4]

automatic rebalancing provision. A variable annuity contract provision that states that values automatically will be transferred between specified accounts to maintain the allocation percentages designated by the contract owner. [2]

Bb

bailout provision. Also known as an *escape clause* or *cash-out provision*. An annuity contract provision that enables the contract owner to surrender the annuity contract, usually without a surrender charge, if renewal interest rates on a fixed annuity fall below a pre-established level, typically 1 percent below the initial interest rate. [2]

before-tax dollars. Money that has not been taxed previously. [7]

beneficiary. The person or legal entity that receives any applicable annuity death benefit. [1]

bond. A type of debt that reflects money the issuer has borrowed and must repay to the bondholder. [4]

bond subaccount. An asset class held by an insurance company's separate account in which deposited funds are typically invested in a variety of both short-term and long-term government and corporate bonds. [4]

branch manager. Under the branch office system, the person who heads a field sales office, recruits, selects, and trains career agents, and acts as the sales manager for the geographic area covered by the sales office. [9]

branch office system. A type of ordinary agency system wherein an insurance company establishes and maintains field sales offices. [9]

brokerage distribution system. A distribution system that relies on the use of agent-brokers and licensed brokers to sell and deliver insurance and annuity products. [9]

broker-dealer. A firm that (1) provides information or advice to its customers regarding the sale and/or purchase of securities, (2) serves as a financial intermediary between buyers and sellers by underwriting or acquiring securities in order to market them to its customers, and (3) supervises the sales process to make sure that sales agents comply with applicable SEC and NASD regulations. [9]

Buyer's Guide to Annuities. A publication that describes the various types of annuities available and some of the annuity features that consumers should consider before purchasing an annuity. [8]

Cc

Canadian Council of Insurance Regulators (CCIR). In Canada, a collective body consisting of the various provincial superintendents of insurance that recommends uniform insurance legislation to the provinces. [8]

cap. An upper limit on the amount of an index's gain in value that will be credited to an equity-indexed annuity contract. [3]

capital appreciation. An increase in the market value of invested assets. [4]

capital gain. The difference between the purchase price and selling price of a piece of property, such as shares in a mutual fund. [5]

career agent. A salesperson who is under contract to at least one insurance company. [9]

cash-out provision. *See* **bailout provision.** [2]

cash surrender value. The accumulated value less any surrender charges included in a policy. [2]

CCIR. *See* **Canadian Council of Insurance Regulators.**

CD. *See* **certificate of deposit.**

certificate of deposit (CD). A contractual agreement issued by a bank that returns the investor's principal with interest on a specified date. [5]

commission. A type of payment for a sales agent's services that is usually based on a specified percentage of the premiums paid on each contract the agent sells. [9]

commutation right. An annuity contract provision governing payout options, which states that the contract owner can withdraw a lump sum from the contract's remaining principal—and any growth of the principal of a variable annuity—even if the contract owner is receiving annuity payments. [10]

compounding. The process by which money earns interest on both the principal *and* the accumulated interest. [5]

compound interest. Interest earned on both the principal *and* the accumulated interest. [5]

comprehensive business analysis. A preliminary review of market conditions and other factors designed to determine the feasibility of any product ideas that appear to meet consumer needs and company objectives. [9]

contingent annuitant. A person who would become the annuitant if the primary annuitant were to die during the accumulation period of an annuity whose contract owner and annuitant are two different persons. [2]

contingent payee. An individual who receives the periodic payments throughout the remainder of the period certain if the payee dies before the period certain has expired. [2]

contract owner. The individual or entity who applies for and purchases an annuity contract. [1]

contract summary. A document that contains relevant contract and benefit information for the specific annuity that a consumer is considering purchasing. [8]

cost recovery rule. A rule governing taxation, which states that withdrawals made from an annuity are considered to be a return of the tax cost basis first and are not considered to be taxable income until after the contract owner withdraws an amount equal to his tax cost basis in the contract. [7]

current interest rate. The interest rate, based on the prevailing interest rates in the economy when an annuity is purchased, that an insurer promises to pay for a specified time period—usually one, three, or five years. [2]

Dd

death benefit guarantee. An annuity contract provision that states if the contract owner dies before the annuity payments begin, then the beneficiary named by the contract owner will receive an annuity benefit equal to the greater of (1) the total amount of premium payments made for the annuity, less any withdrawals made, or (2) the accumulated value at the time of the contract owner's death. [2]

deferred annuity. An annuity under which periodic payments generally are scheduled to begin more than one annuity period after the date on which the annuity was purchased. [1]

deferred profit sharing plan (DPSP). A Canadian retirement program under which plan sponsor contributions are related to profits and are tax deductible by the plan sponsor, subject to specified maximum annual deductible amounts. [7]

defined benefit plan. A type of pension plan that specifies the amount of benefit—based on the employee's income, years of service, or both income and years of service—a participant will receive at retirement. [6]

defined contribution plan. Also known as a *money purchase plan*. A type of pension plan that specifies the annual contribution the employer will deposit into the plan on behalf of each plan participant. [6]

direct response distribution system. A sales distribution system wherein the consumer purchases products directly from a company by responding to the company's advertisements or telephone solicitations. [9]

distribution. The activities that sellers engage in to make products available for consumers to buy. [9]

distribution channel. *See* **distribution system.**

distribution system. Also known as a *distribution channel.* A method of transferring products from a manufacturer—in this case an insurance company—to consumers. [9]

diversification. The process of investing in a number of financial instru-ments within an asset class in order to minimize the risk associated with any one investment or type of investment. [4]

dividend. A stockowner's share of a company's profits. [4]

dollar cost averaging. The process of investing a fixed dollar amount in one or more financial instruments on a regular, periodic basis. [4]

DPSP. *See* **deferred profit sharing plan.**

Ee

entire contract provision. A contract provision common to all types of con-tracts that specifies that only those documents attached to or appearing in the contract constitute the contract. [2]

equity-indexed annuity. A type of annuity that offers the same type of interest rate guarantees as a traditional fixed annuity, but also may credit additional interest depending upon the performance of the stock market. [3]

escape clause. *See* **bailout provision.**

exchange. An activity wherein one party—a buyer—gives something of value to another party—a seller—in order to receive something of value in return. [9]

exclusion ratio. A formula used to calculate the portion of each annuity payment that an owner can exclude from his taxable income. [7]

Ff

FDIC. *See* **Federal Deposit Insurance Corporation.**

Federal Deposit Insurance Corporation (FDIC). In the United States, a federal agency that guarantees funds on deposit in member financial institutions. [5]

fixed account. Also known as a *variable guaranteed account.* A variable annuity subaccount that guarantees payment of a fixed rate of interest for a specified period of time. [4]

fixed amount. An annuity payout option under which the insurer determines the length of time that the annuity's accumulated value will provide a preselected periodic payment. [2]

fixed annuity. An annuity for which the insurer guarantees to pay a specified rate of interest on the accumulated value for a specified period of time. [1]

fixed payout. A type of annuity payment, which guarantees that the payment will remain the same during the payout period. [2]

fixed period. An annuity payout option under which the insurer makes annuity payments for a specified period of time. [2]

flexible-premium annuity. An annuity for which the contract owner pays premiums, which can vary between a set minimum amount and a set maximum amount, on a periodic basis over a stated period of time. [1]

free look provision. An annuity contract provision that states that the contract owner has a period of time—usually 10 to 20 days—to examine the annuity contract, with the option of returning it to the insurer for a full refund of the premium or, in some states, for a refund of the market value of a variable annuity. [2]

free withdrawal provision. An annuity contract provision that grants the contract owner the right to withdraw all or a portion of the annuity's accumulated value during the accumulation period. [2]

fund transfer. A special service that provides for the movement of funds between variable annuity investment subaccounts during the accumulation phase as well as during the payout period. [4]

future value (FV). An amount of money that has been invested plus the interest earned over a certain period of time. [5]

FV. *See* **future value.**

Gg

general account. The general fund of assets invested to support an insurer's traditional insurance products. [1]

general agency system. A type of ordinary agency system wherein general agents establish and maintain field sales offices for an insurance company. [9]

general agent. An independent business person who is under contract to an insurance company and is given the power to represent the insurance company and to develop new business within a geographically defined area. [9]

gross estate. The total value of property subject to estate taxes. [7]

guaranteed interest rate. The interest rate—typically 3 or 4 percent—that the insurance company specifies that it will pay on a fixed annuity's principal balance for the duration of the annuity contract. [2]

guaranty association. In the United States, an agency that is composed of all the life insurance companies operating in a state and that is established to cover the financial obligations of member companies that go out of business. [8]

Hh

high water mark method. A method for crediting excess interest to an equity-indexed annuity that involves comparing the value of the index at the beginning of the term of the contract with the highest value that the index reaches at certain points, usually contract anniversary dates, during the term. [3]

Ii

immediate annuity. An annuity for which payments generally are scheduled to begin one year after the date on which the annuity was purchased. [1]

income date. Also known as the *maturity date* or the *annuity date*. The date on which the insurer begins to make annuity payments. [2]

income tax. A tax that is levied on income that a person or business earns. [7]

incontestability provision. An annuity provision, which states that after the contract becomes effective, the insurer generally cannot contest it. [2]

index. A statistical measurement system that tracks the performance of a group of similar investments. [3]

individual retirement account. *See* **individual retirement arrangement (IRA).** [6]

individual retirement annuity. *See* **individual retirement arrangement (IRA).** [6]

individual retirement arrangement (IRA). Also known as an *individual retirement account* or *individual retirement annuity*. In the United States, an arrangement that allows people with earned income to deposit a portion of that income in a tax-deferred savings plan. [6]

inflation risk. The risk that the average level of prices for goods and services will increase during an investment period. [5]

Insurance Companies Act. The primary federal law that governs insurance companies operating in Canada. [8]

interest. The fees that bond issuers, banks, and other financial institutions pay for the use of borrowed money. [4]

interest first rule. A rule governing taxation, which states that any amount the contract owner takes out of an annuity will be considered a withdrawal of the interest (which has not been taxed), until the contract owner has withdrawn all of the interest in the contract. [7]

interest rate risk. The chance that unpredictable fluctuations in interest rates will jeopardize the opportunity to maximize the return on an investment. [5]

investment adviser. A firm or person who is compensated in exchange for providing advice to investors about the value of securities and the potential advantages and disadvantages of buying and selling securities. [8]

Investment Advisers Act of 1940. In the United States, a federal law that regulates the conduct of investment advisers. [8]

investment company. A company that issues securities and engages primarily in investing and trading securities. [8]

Investment Company Act of 1940. In the United States, a federal law that regulates the conduct of investment companies. [8]

IRA. *See* **individual retirement arrangement.**

Jj

joint and survivor annuity. A type of annuity that provides a series of periodic payments to more than one person, and those payments continue until the death of the last surviving annuitant. [1]

joint annuitant. An individual who is named in the contract with the annuitant, and whose age and life expectancy are also used in the calculations to determine what the annuity payments will be. [1]

joint owner. A person who shares ownership of an annuity contract with the contract owner and, in some types of joint ownership, would have the same right as the contract owner to approve any decisions made about the contract. [2]

Kk

Keogh plan. In the United States, an arrangement that allows self-employed persons to deposit a portion of their income earned from self-employment in a tax-deferred savings plan. [6]

Ll

licensed broker. A salesperson who is not under an agency contract with any insurance company and who is acting as an agent of the buyer. [9]

life annuity. An annuity that provides periodic payments for at least the lifetime of the annuitant. [2]

life income with period certain annuity. A type of annuity that guarantees that payments will be made throughout the annuitant's lifetime, but also guarantees that the payments will be made for at least a certain period, even if the annuitant dies before the end of that period. [1]

life income with refund annuity. Also known as a *refund annuity*. An annuity that provides payments throughout the lifetime of the annuitant and guarantees that at least the purchase price of the annuity will be paid out. [2]

location selling distribution system. A distribution system wherein an insurer sets up an office or installs an information kiosk in a retail store, a shopping mall, or a bank or other financial institution in order to attract customers for insurance and annuity products. [9]

lump sum distribution. A payout option by which a contract owner receives the balance of his account in a single payment. [2]

Mm

market. A group of people who, either as individuals or as members of organizations, are the actual or potential buyers of a product. [9]

market analysis. A study of all the environmental factors that might affect sales of a product. [9]

market conduct. The manner in which an insurer carries out its various business activities. [8]

marketing. The process of planning and executing product development, pricing, promotion, and distribution in order to create exchanges that satisfy the needs and objectives of both buyers and sellers. [9]

marketing mix. The four major factors that a company considers when determining how best to meet consumer needs: product, price, promotion, and distribution. [9]

marketing plan. A plan that specifies a company's overall marketing objectives, the strategies needed to achieve those objectives, and the specific sales goals for each product or line of products a company offers. [9]

market risk. The risk associated with fluctuations in stock prices. [5]

market segmentation. The process of dividing the total market for a product into groups of consumers who share common needs or characteristics. [9]

market segments. Groups of consumers who share common needs or characteristics. [9]

market value adjusted annuity. An annuity that features fixed interest rate guarantees combined with an interest rate adjustment factor that can cause the actual rate credited to fluctuate in response to market conditions. [4]

maturity date. *See* **income date.**

McCarran-Ferguson Act. Federal legislation enacted in 1945 under which the U.S. Congress agreed to leave insurance regulation to the states as long as it considered state regulation to be adequate. [8]

M&E charge. *See* **mortality and expense risks charge.**

minimum distribution. The specified amount that a traditional IRA owner or qualified retirement plan participant must receive from his accounts by a specified age or time. [7]

MLA system. *See* multiple-line agency system.

model law. Sample legislation developed by the National Association of Insurance Commissioners (NAIC) that state legislatures can adopt into law exactly as written or use as a basis for developing their own legislation. [8]

money market subaccount. An asset class held by an insurance company's separate account in which deposited funds are typically invested in short-term money instruments or cash equivalents, such as United States Treasury bills. [4]

money purchase plan. *See* **defined contribution plan.**

mortality and expense risks (M&E) charge. A fee ranging from 1 to 1.75 percent of the variable annuity contract value that provides for payment of a death benefit, ensures that the expense risks charged on the contract won't increase, covers a guaranteed interest rate paid on one type of variable annuity subaccount, and may cover the overhead expenses the insurer incurs with respect to the annuity contract. [2]

multiple-line agency (MLA) system. A distribution system that uses career agents to market all of the life, health, annuity, and property/casualty products offered by groups of financially interrelated or commonly managed insurance companies. [9]

mutual fund. An account established by a financial services company that combines the money of many people and invests it in a variety of financial instruments. [4]

Nn

NAIC. *See* **National Association of Insurance Commissioners.**

NASD. *See* **National Association of Securities Dealers.**

National Association of Insurance Commissioners (NAIC). In the United States, a private, nonprofit organization consisting of the insurance commissioners or superintendents of the various state insurance departments. [8]

National Association of Securities Dealers (NASD). In the United States, a nonprofit organization of securities dealers responsible for regulating the market conduct of member companies and representatives. [8]

nonagency building system. A type of sales distribution system wherein companies generally recruit salespeople who require little training, are financially self-supporting, and operate out of independent office facilities. [9]

nonforfeiture provision. A contract provision required in individual deferred fixed annuity contracts, which states that if the contract owner stops making premium payments, he will still receive an annuity benefit based on the amount of premiums he has paid. If the annuity contract provides for a lump sum settlement, the contract must also provide that, on surrender of the contract during the accumulation period, the insurer will pay a lump sum to the contract owner in lieu of an annuity benefit. [2]

non-natural owner. The owner of an annuity contract that is not a person but is an entity such as a trust, a partnership, or a corporation. [1]

nonqualified annuity. A type of annuity that has few limitations on the amount of premium that can be invested but that does not receive all of the tax advantages afforded qualified annuities. [1]

Oo

Office of the Superintendent of Financial Institutions (OSFI). The federal agency that is responsible for monitoring the operations of all financial institutions in Canada, including life insurance companies. [8]

Office of the Superintendent of Insurance. In Canada, an administrative agency established by each province to enforce the province's insurance laws and regulations. [8]

ordinary agency system. A distribution system that uses full-time career agents and agent-brokers to sell and deliver insurance and annuity products. [9]

OSFI. *See* **Office of the Superintendent of Financial Institutions.**

Pp

participation rate. The percentage of a specified index's gain in value that will be credited to an equity-indexed annuity contract. [3]

payee. The person who receives the annuity payments. [1]

payout option provision. Also known as the *settlement option provision.* In an annuity contract, a list that describes each of the payout options from which the contract owner may select. [2]

payout period. The period during which the payee receives payments. [1]

Pension Benefits Act. In Canada, legislation enacted by the federal and provincial governments that governs the terms and operation of private retirement plans. [6]

pension plan. An agreement under which an employer establishes a plan to provide its employees with a lifetime monthly income benefit that begins at retirement. [6]

period certain. The stated period over which the insurer will make annuity payments. [2]

personal-producing general agency (PPGA) system. A distribution system that relies on personal-producing general agents to sell and deliver insurance and annuity products. [9]

personal-producing general agent. A commissioned sales agent who typically works alone, is not housed in an insurance company field office, and engages primarily in personal selling. [9]

personal selling. A promotional tool that relies on salespersons to present product information during face-to-face meetings with one or more prospective buyers. [9]

personal selling distribution system. A sales distribution system that uses commissioned or salaried salespersons to sell products through oral and written presentations to consumers. [9]

plan participants. Employees who are covered by the private retirement plans established by their employers. [6]

plan sponsors. Employers that establish private retirement plans. [6]

plan trustee. One who holds legal title to a retirement plan's assets on behalf of the plan participants. [6]

point-to-point method. A method for crediting excess interest to an equity-indexed annuity that involves comparing the value of the index at the start of the annuity contract term to its value at the end of the term to determine what, if any, excess interest has accrued because of a change in the index. [3]

portfolio. A diversified collection of securities that aligns specific investment strategies with an investor's personal financial goals. [4]

PPGA. *See* **personal-producing general agency system.**

premature distributions. Withdrawals of earnings from an annuity made before the contract owner is age 59½. [7]

present value (PV). The amount of money that must be invested today in order to accumulate a specified amount of money by a certain date. [5]

price. An item of value that a buyer gives to a seller in exchange for a product; typically, price refers to an amount of money. [9]

principal. The total amount the contract owner has invested in an annuity, exclusive of any investment returns [3]; in an agent contract, a party that authorizes another party, known as the agent, to perform certain acts on its behalf. [9]

product. A good, service, or idea that a seller offers to buyers in order to satisfy their needs. [9]

product design objectives. A list, compiled by a product development team, that specifies a product's basic characteristics, features, benefits, and the manner in which the benefits will be provided. [9]

profit sharing plan. A type of employer-sponsored retirement plan that is funded primarily by employer contributions payable from, and usually based on, the employer's profits. [6]

promotion. The activities that sellers use to communicate with buyers in order to influence them to purchase a product. [9]

prospectus. A written document describing specific aspects of a security being offered for sale. [8]

publicity. A form of promotion that provides information about a company or its products and services, and is transmitted in a news format by the mass media. [9]

PV. *See* **present value.**

Qq

qualified annuity. An annuity that is purchased to either fund or distribute funds from a tax-qualified plan and is exempt from current income taxation during the accumulation period. [1]

Rr

ratchet method. *See* **annual reset method.**

readability requirements. Laws that require insurers to reduce the amount of technical jargon and legal language included in insurance and annuity contracts. [8]

refund annuity. *See* **life income with refund annuity.**

registered pension plan (RPP). In Canada, an employee benefit plan—such as a retirement plan—that satisfies legal requirements to receive certain federal tax benefits. [6]

registered representative. A sales representative or other person who has registered with the National Association of Securities Dealers (NASD), disclosed the required background information, and passed one or more NASD examination. [8]

registered retirement savings plan (RRSP). A Canadian retirement account, similar to individual retirement accounts in the United States, that allows individuals or their spouses (not employers) to make tax-deductible contributions, subject to specified maximum deductible amounts. [7]

renewal rate. The new interest rate that an insurer declares for a subsequent period when the current interest rate time period ends. The renewal rate may be higher or lower than the current interest rate, depending upon conditions in the general economy and how the insurer has invested the funds. [2]

return. The profit or compensation an investor earns for taking a risk. [4]

risk. The possibility of loss. [4]

risk-return trade-off. The interplay between risk and return, which usually results in higher risks generating higher returns, and lower risks generating lower returns. [4]

rollover. An employee's transfer of retirement funds from one qualified plan to another plan of the same type or to an IRA without incurring any tax liability. [7]

RRSP. *See* **registered retirement savings plan.**

Ss

salaried sales distribution system. A distribution system that relies on the use of a company's salaried sales representatives to sell and service all types of insurance and annuity products. [9]

salaried sales representatives. Employees of the insurer who are paid on a salary basis to sell and service all types of insurance and annuity products. [9]

sales promotion. A type of incentive that a company offers to encourage salespersons to sell a product or to encourage consumers to purchase a product. [9]

Savings Incentive Match Plan for Employees (SIMPLE) 401(k). In the United States, a special arrangement whereby an employer with 100 or fewer employees can establish a simplified 401(k) retirement savings plan for employees. [6]

Savings Incentive Match Plan for Employees (SIMPLE) IRA. In the United States, a special arrangement whereby an employer with 100 or fewer employees can establish a simplified retirement savings plan for employees. [6]

screening process. A step in the product development process wherein the product development team quickly scrutinizes product ideas and weeds out those ideas that are not consistent with an insurer's current or future marketing plans. [9]

SEC. *See* **Securities and Exchange Commission.**

Securities Act of 1933. In the United States, a federal law that protects investors by requiring that they receive specified types of information about securities being offered for sale to the public. [8]

Securities and Exchange Commission (SEC). An agency of the U.S. government charged with regulating transactions in financial securities. [4]

Securities Exchange Act of 1934. In the United States, a federal law that created the Securities and Exchange Commission (SEC) and granted it broad authority to regulate the securities industry. [8]

segregated account. In Canada, an investment account maintained separately from an insurer's general account to help manage the funds placed in variable insurance products such as variable annuities. [1]

separate account. In the United States, an investment account maintained separately from an insurer's general account to help manage the funds placed in variable insurance products such as variable annuities. [1]

SEP plan. *See* **simplified employee pension plan.**

settlement option. *See* **payout option provision.**

SIMPLE 401(k). *See* **Savings Incentive Match Plan for Employees 401(k).**

SIMPLE IRA. *See* **Savings Incentive Match Plan for Employees IRA.**

simplified employee pension (SEP) plan. In the United States, a qualified employer-sponsored pension plan arrangement whereby an employer establishes and makes contributions into an IRA for each participating employee. [6]

single-premium annuity. An annuity that is purchased by the payment of one lump–sum premium. [1]

single-premium deferred annuity (SPDA). An annuity purchased with a single premium whose payments generally do not begin within the annuity period, for example within the next month or next year. [1]

single-premium immediate annuity (SPIA). An annuity whose payments begin soon after it is purchased with a single premium. [1]

solvency. The ability of an insurer to make specified payments to contract owners and to meet other financial obligations on time. [8]

SPDA. *See* **single-premium deferred annuity.**

special services. Contract provisions designed to help variable annuity contract owners more efficiently manage their variable subaccount investments. [4]

specialty advertising. A form of consumer sales promotion that uses articles imprinted with a company name or logo, address, phone number, and sometimes a sales message to promote the company, its salespeople, or its products. [9]

SPIA. *See* **single-premium immediate annuity.**

stagnant market risk. The risk that the stock market will experience neither a significant gain nor a significant loss. [5]

state insurance department. In the United States, an administrative agency that is charged with assuring that insurance companies operating within a state comply with all of that state's insurance laws and regulations. [8]

stock subaccount. An asset class held by an insurance company's separate account in which deposited funds are typically invested in an array of domestic and foreign stocks. [4]

stock. An ownership share in a company. [4]

straight life annuity. A type of annuity that provides periodic payments only for as long as the annuitant lives. Upon the death of the annuitant, the insurer has no further responsibility under the annuity contract. [1]

subaccount. Also known as a *variable investment account* or a *variable subaccount.* An investment fund that allows the insurer to place variable annuity premiums in a wide variety of investment options. [1]

surrender charge. A penalty for prematurely withdrawing funds from an annuity. [2]

surrender. A type of withdrawal that involves withdrawing an annuity contract's entire accumulated value less any surrender charges included in the policy. [2]

Tt

target market. A market segment on which a company focuses its marketing efforts. [9]

target marketing. The process of evaluating various market segments and then selecting one or more market segment—called a target market—on which to focus the company's marketing efforts. [9]

tax cost basis. The amount of money contributed to an annuity that will not be subject to taxation because it has already been taxed. [7]

tax-qualified plan. An employer-sponsored retirement plan that satisfies the complex legal requirements of the Internal Revenue Code and ERISA and, as a result, provides certain favorable tax treatments for both the employer and employee. [1]

Tax Sheltered Annuity (TSA). A retirement annuity sold only to public school teachers and employees of hospitals, colleges, and other organizations offering qualified retirement plans under section 403(b) of the U.S. Internal Revenue Code. [6]

term. The length of time over which the interest to be credited to an annuity contract will be calculated. [3]

time value of money. The concept that the value of a sum of money will change over time as the result of the effect of interest. [5]

transfers. A special service that allows contract owners to move assets between variable annuity subaccounts during the accumulation phase as well as during the payout period. [4]

trustee transfer. A rollover of retirement funds under which the current plan transfers the money directly to the new plan—or, in the case of an IRA, to the company that has custody of the account. [7]

TSA. *See* **Tax Sheltered Annuity.**

Vv

variable annuity. An annuity under which the amount of the policy's accumulated value and the amount of the periodic annuity payments fluctuate in accordance with the performance of a specified pool of investments. [1]

variable guaranteed account. *See* **fixed account.**

variable investment account. *See* **subaccount.**

variable payout option. A variable annuity payout option whereby the insurer pays the annuitant a series of annuity payments that vary throughout the payout period based on the performance of the underlying subaccounts. [2]

variable subaccount. *See* **subaccount.**

vesting schedule. A timetable that specifies how much a contract owner can withdraw—before the end of the contract term—of the gain in the index's value that has been credited to an equity-indexed annuity contract. [3]

Ww

waiver of premium for disability rider. An annuity contract provision that allows the contract owner to stop making premium payments in the event that he becomes disabled. [2]

waiver of surrender charge provision. A contract provision, which states that the insurer will not subject a withdrawal to a surrender charge under certain specified conditions. [2]

window premiums. Additional premiums paid on a single-premium deferred annuity during the first contract year. [1]

INDEX

Aa

accumulated value, 10
accumulation period, 8
accumulation units, 21, 44–46
administrative fee, 21
advertising, 104–105, 109, 121
after-tax dollars, 87–88
agency building systems, 124
agency contract, 123
agent, 123
agent-broker, 124
AIR. *See* assumed investment return
annual annuity, 7
annual reset method, 36
Annual Return, 112
Annual Statement, 100
annuitant, 5, 6
  death of, 25
  maximum age of, 16
annuitization, 26–28, 140
annuity
  compared to other financial products, 66–69
  contract, 15–30
  defined, 3
  future of market, 131–141

issuers of, 3, 5–6
life insurance products vs., 4
marketing and distributing, 115–128
regulation of, 99–112, 137–138
sellers of, 3, 5
taxation of, 85–96
terms of contract, 5
types of, 7–11
uses for, 4–5
See also specific types of annuities.
annuity certain, 26
annuity contract, 5, 15–30
  accumulation period, 19–25
  applicant information, 16
  contract ownership, 16–17
  contract provisions, 17–18, 104, 139–140
  free look provision, 19
  parties to, 5–7
  payout period, 25–30
  process of applying for, 15–19
  purchase payments, 18–19
annuity date, 25
annuity market
  current environment for, 3–4, 11
  future of, 131–141
annuity period, 7

annuity taxation, 85–96
annuity units, 53
applicant information, 16
application, 16
asset allocation, 48–50, 65
asset allocation model, 49
asset class, 47
asset management fee, 22
assignment provision, 17, 93
assumed investment return, 54–55
automatic dollar cost averaging, 50–51
automatic rebalancing provision, 21

Bb

bailout provision, 24
before-tax dollars, 85
beneficiary, 5, 7
bond subaccount, 47
bonds, 47, 48, 69
branch manager, 124
branch office system, 124
brokerage distribution system, 126
broker-dealer, 126
Buyer's Guide to Annuities, 105

Cc

Canadian Council of Insurance Regulators, 110
Canadian regulation, 110–112
cap, 37
capital appreciation, 46–47
capital gain, 67
capital gains tax, 137
career agent, 124, 125
cash-out provision, 24
cash surrender value, 23
CCIR. *See* Canadian Council of Insurance Regulators
CD. *See* certificate of deposit.
certificate of deposit, 59
charges. *See* fees
commission, 124
commutation right, 139

compound interest, 64
compounding, 64
comprehensive business analysis, 118–119
contingent annuitant, 17
contingent payee, 26, 27
contract, 15–16. *See also* annuity contract
contract forms, 103
contract owner, 5, 6
    death of, 25
    naming of beneficiary, 7
contract ownership, 16–17
contract provisions, 17–18, 38, 103, 104, 139–140
contract summary, 105
cost recovery rule, 91
current interest rate, 20

Dd

death benefit
    guarantee, 25
    provisions, 25
    on variable annuities, 52
deferred annuity, 8, 9
    accumulation period in, 19
    payout guarantees, 34–35
deferred profit sharing plan, 96
defined benefit plan, 77–78
defined contribution plan, 77–78
direct marketing, 140–141
direct response distribution system, 123, 126–127
disclosure, 108–109
disclosure requirements, 105
distribution, 115
distribution channel. *See* distribution systems.
distribution systems, 122–128
    direct response, 123, 126–127
    personal selling, 123–126
    choosing, 127–128
diversification, 47, 65
dividend, 47
dollar cost averaging, 50–51, 64–65

Ee

education funding, 74–75
education IRA, 74
Employee Income Retirement
    Security Act, 10, 75–76, 85, 86,
    88
employer-sponsored pension plans,
    135–136
employer-sponsored retirement
    plans, annuities and, 138
entire contract provision, 17
equity-indexed annuity, 35–38
    contract provisions, 38
    defined, 33
    excess interest, calculating, 36–37
    excess interest, crediting, 37–38
    growth of market, 38
    index, 35–37
    interest rate guarantees, 36
    investment risk and return, 41–
        42
    personal selling for, 123
    pricing, 38
    risk and, 62–63
ERISA. *See* Employee Income
    Retirement Security Act
escape clause, 24
estate taxes, 93–94
excess interest, 36–38
exchange, 115
exclusion ratio, 89

Ff

FDIC. *See* Federal Deposit
    Insurance Corporation
Federal Deposit Insurance
    Corporation, 66
federal regulation
    Canada, 111–112
    U.S., 105–109
federal securities regulation,
    exemption from, 109–110
fees, 21–22
fixed account, 43–44

fixed amount option, 26
fixed annuity, 10–11, 33–35
    general account, 33–34
    inflation erosion, 35
    interest rate guarantees, 33–34
    investment risk and return, 41–
        42
    payout guarantees, 34–35
    premium payments, 20–21
    purchase payments, 19
    risk and, 62–63
fixed payout option, 28, 53
fixed period option, 26
fixed and variable payout option,
    on variable annuities, 54
flexible-premium annuity, 9
401(k) plan, 78–79, 87, 135–136,
    138
403(b) plan, 79, 87, 138
457 plan, 79
free look provision, 19
free withdrawal provision, 23
future value, 64
FV. *See* future value.

Gg

general account, 11, 33–34, 42–43
general agency system, 124
general agent, 124–125
gross estate, 94
group annuity, 10, 16. *See also*
    group retirement plans
group retirement plans, 75–82
guaranteed interest rate, 20
guaranty association, 101–102

Hh

high water mark method, 36–37

Ii

immediate annuity, 7, 9, 34
income date, 25
income tax, 85–93

annuity income taxation, 89–93
deductibility of premium payments for IRA and nonqualified annuity owners, 87–88
deductibility of premium payments for plan participant, 86–87
deductibility of premium payments for sponsors of qualified retirement plans, 88
tax deferral on investment income, 85–86
Income Tax Act, 95
incontestability provision, 17–18
index, 35–37, 55
individual annuities, 10, 95
individual deferred fixed annuity contracts, nonforfeiture provision in, 18
individual nonqualified annuities, 71–75
individual retirement account. *See* individual retirement arrangements
individual retirement annuity. *See* individual retirement arrangements
individual retirement arrangements, 72–73, 74
inflation erosion, 35
inflation risk, 63
Insurance Companies Act, 111–112
insurer, role in annuity transaction, 5–6
interest, 47
interest first rule, 91
interest rate guarantees, 33–34, 36
interest rate risk, 62–63
interest rates, 20–21
Internal Revenue Code (U.S.), 10, 75–76, 78–79, 85, 86
Internal Revenue Service, 136
investment adviser, 106
Investment Advisers Act of 1940, 106

investment company, 106
Investment Company Act of 1940, 106
investment principles, 64–65
investment return, 42
investment risk, 41–42
IRA. *See* individual retirement arrangement

Jj

joint annuitant, 7
joint owner, 17
joint and survivor annuity, 11, 27–28

Kk

Keogh plan, 79–80

Ll

licensed broker, 126
life annuity, 27
life cycle investment strategies, 61
life income with period certain, 27
life income with period certain annuity, 11
life income with refund annuity, 27
loans
    nonqualified annuities and, 93
    qualified annuities and, 92–93
location selling distribution system, 125
lump sum distribution, 26, 73–74

Mm

M&E charge. *See* mortality and expense risks charge
market, 116
market analysis, 118
market conduct regulation
    Canada, 111
    U.S., 100, 102–103

market risk, 63–64
market segmentation, 116
market segments, 116
market value adjusted annuity, 55–56, 123
marketing, 115–116
marketing mix, 115
marketing plan, 116
maturity date, 25
McCarran-Ferguson Act, 99
minimum distribution, 92
misstatement of age or sex, 18
model law, 100, 101
money market accounts, 48
money market subaccount, 47
money purchase plan. *See* defined contribution plan
monthly annuity, 7
mortality and expense risks charge, 22
multiple-line agency system, 125
mutual funds, 44
    annuities compared to, 67–69
    compared to after-tax annuities, 68

Nn

NAIC Model Annuity and Deposit Fund Disclosure Regulation, 105
NAIC Replacement of Life Insurance and Annuities Model Regulation, 103
NAIC Rules Governing the Advertising of Life Insurance, 104
NASD. *See* National Association of Securities Dealers
National Association of Insurance Commissioners, 99–101. *See also NAIC listings*
National Association of Securities Dealers, 106–107, 137
NationsBank of N.C. v. Variable Annuity Life Insurance Company (VALIC), 125–126

nonagency building system, 126
nondiscrimination, 75
nonforfeiture provision, 18
non-natural owner, 6
nonqualified annuities, 10, 71
nonqualified retirement plans, 81

Oo

Office of the Superintendent of Financial Institutions, 112
Office of the Superintendent of Insurance, 110–111
ordinary agency system, 124–125
OSFI. *See* Office of the Superintendent of Financial Institutions

Pp

participation, 75
participation rate, 37
payee, 5
payment calculations, 28–30
payout guarantees, 34–35
payout option provision, 25–26
payout options, variable annuities, 52–53
payout period, 8
payout period options, 11
payout period, on variable annuities, 52–55
Pension Benefits Act, 76
pension plans, 77–78
period certain, 26
personal selling, 120
personal selling distribution system, 122–126
personal-producing general agency system, 126
personal-producing general agent, 126
plan participants, 75
plan sponsors, 75
plan trustee, 76
point-to-point method, 37

population, aging of, 4
portfolio, 49
premature distributions, 92
premium payments, 19–21
present value, 64
price, 115
principal (in an agency contract), 123
principal (of an annuity), 33, 46
product, 115
product design objectives, 118–119
product development, 116–120
product implementation, 119–120
product planning, 117–118
product promotion, 120–122
product review, 120
product technical design, 119
profit sharing plan, 78
promotion, 115
prospectus, 108
provincial regulation, 110–111
publicity, 121–122
purchase payments, 18–19
PV. *See* present value

Qq

qualified annuity, 10, 24, 71
qualified retirement plans, 76–79

Rr

ratchet method, 36
readability requirements, 103
refund annuity, 27
registered pension plan, 76, 96
registered representatives, 107
registered retirement savings plans, 96
regulation, 99–112
  advertising and disclosure requirements, 104–105
  Canadian, 110–112
  equity-indexed annuities, 109–110
  federal (U.S.) regulation, 105–109

market value annuities, 109–110
  state regulation, 99–103
renewal rate, 20
retirees, growing number of, 131
retirement funding, 3, 4–5, 23, 71–72
retirement, lengthening of, 133
retirement planning, 134
retirement plans, 95–96
retirement savings plans, 78–79
return, 41
risk, 41
  dealing with, 59–64
  equity-indexed annuities and, 62–63
  fixed annuities and, 62–63
  variable annuities and, 63–64
risk-return trade-off, 49, 59–62
risk tolerance, investing and, 60–62
rollovers, 73, 94–95
Roth IRA, 72–75, 87, 92

Ss

salaried sales distribution system, 125
salaried sales representative, 125
sales agent, 124
sales monitoring, 120
sales promotion, 121
savings accounts, 66–67
Savings Incentive Match Plan for Employees (SIMPLE) IRA, 80–81
screening process, 118
SEC. *See* Securities and Exchange Commission
Section 1035 Exchanges, 94
Securities Act of 1933, 105–106
Securities Exchange Act of 1934, 105–106
Securities and Exchange Commission, 42, 105–106, 107, 108, 138
segregated account, 11
SEP. *See* simplified employee pension plan
separate account, 11, 42–43

settlement option provision, 25–26
SIMPLE (Savings Incentive Match Plan for Employees) 401(k), 81
SIMPLE (Savings Incentive Match Plan for Employees) plans, 80–82, 136
simplified employee pension plan, 80, 136
single-premium annuity, 8–9
single-premium deferred annuity, 9
single-premium immediate annuity, 8–9, 25
Social Security system, 3–4, 132–135, 138
solvency, 100
solvency regulation
  Canada, 110–111
  U.S., 100–102
SPDA. *See* single-premium deferred annuity.
special services, 49–51
specialty advertising, 121
SPIA. *See* single-premium individual annuity.
stagnant market risk, 63
state insurance department, 99
state licensing, 102–103
state regulation, 99–103
  market conduct, 102–103
  solvency, 100–102
stock market, 4
stocks, 47, 48, 69
stock subaccount, 47
straight life annuity, 11, 27
subaccount, 11, 21, 43–48
  accumulation units, 44–46
  asset classes, 46–47
  automatic rebalancing, 51–52
  investment options, 47–48
  transfers between, 51
  types of, 47
suitability, 107–108
surrender, 23
surrender charge, 22, 23–24

Tt

target market, 116
target marketing, 116

taxation of annuities, 23, 85–96
  Canada, 95–96
  United States, 85–95
taxation requirements, source of, 86
tax cost basis, 88
tax-qualified plan, 10
tax reform, regulation of annuities and, 136–137
Tax Sheltered Annuity, 79
1035 exchanges, 137
term, 36
time value of money, 64
traditional IRA, 72–75, 87, 92
transfers, 51
trustee transfer, 95
TSA. *See* Tax Sheltered Annuity

Uu

unisex mortality tables, 16

Vv

variable annuities, 4, 11, 41–55
  advertising, 109
  annual report of separate account activity, 109
  asset allocation, 48–50
  charges, reduction and elimination of, 139
  death benefit, 52
  fees on, 22
  free look provision in, 19
  investment options, 47–48
  investment risk and return, 41–42
  no interest rate guarantee, 36
  payout period, 52–55
  premium payments, 21
  purchase payments, 19
  risk and, 63–64
  separate account, 42–43
  special services, 49–51
  subaccounts, 19, 43–48
variable guaranteed account. *See* fixed account
variable investment account. *See* subaccount

variable payout option, 28, 53–54
variable subaccount. *See*
    subaccount
vesting, 75
vesting schedule, 37–38

Ww–Zz

waiver of premium for disability
    rider, 18
waiver of surrender charge
    provision, 23–24
window premium, 9
withdrawal penalties, 72–73
withdrawals, 23–25, 91–92